I have never read a more powerful an healing odyssey that is not only pure in_ healing power of self-love. Denise DeSin on the spiritual path who must reconcile tne impertection of the human condition with the principle of innate wholeness. She so eloquently shares how to transform an evil into good, a disease into a teacher, and reveals what is possible when the path of healing includes the discovery of one's innate well-being and true worth.

Gary Simmons, Th.D.
author of *The I of the Storm, The Soul's Conspiracy,*
and co-author of The Art & Practice of Living with
Nothing and No One Against You

Inspiring, uplifting and truly illuminating! The scope and magnitude of *From Stage IV to Center Stage* is astounding. Combining traditional allopathic medicine with alternative health practices, Denise DeSimone chronicles her journey through cancer in a gut wrenching and heart warming way. Through her experience with a life threatening illness, she overcame what for many would seem the impossible; yet she not only survived—she thrived! The ultimate message that Denise shares is the healing power of self-love. This book is a must read for all those who face challenges in their lives.

Andi & Jonathan Goldman
authors of *Chakra Frequencies*

Oral, head and neck cancer challenges the patient, the family, and the caregiver. *From Stage IV to Center Stage is* a book that exemplifies the powerful healing capacity that family, friends, and community encourage. Embracing throat cancer, and sharing her story, is a guiding light for others who face the same diagnosis. The choices Denise made expands the options for those dealing with head and neck cancer. This is a book to which many survivors will identify.

Nancy Leupold
President and founder of SPOHNC –
Support for People with Oral Head and Neck Cancer

FROM STAGE IV TO CENTER STAGE

Denise DeSimone

BALBOA.
PRESS
A DIVISION OF HAY HOUSE

Balboa Press books may be ordered through booksellers or by contacting:

Balboa Press
A Division of Hay House
1663 Liberty Drive
Bloomington, IN 47403
www.balboapress.com
1-(877) 407-4847

Because of the dynamic nature of the Internet, any web addresses or links contained in this book may have changed since publication and may no longer be valid. The views expressed in this work are solely those of the author and do not necessarily reflect the views of the publisher, and the publisher hereby disclaims any responsibility for them.

The author of this book does not dispense medical advice or prescribe the use of any technique as a form of treatment for physical, emotional, or medical problems without the advice of a physician, either directly or indirectly. The intent of the author is only to offer information of a general nature to help you in your quest for emotional and spiritual well-being. In the event you use any of the information in this book for yourself, which is your constitutional right, the author and the publisher assume no responsibility for your actions.

Any people depicted in stock imagery provided by Thinkstock are models, and such images are being used for illustrative purposes only.
Certain stock imagery © Thinkstock.

ISBN: 978-1-4525-3537-1 (sc)
ISBN: 978-1-4525-3539-5 (hc)
ISBN: 978-1-4525-3538-8 (e)

Library of Congress Control Number: 2011909468

Printed in the United States of America

Balboa Press rev. date: 06/21/2011

For Caregivers

CONTENTS

Foreword ix
Acknowledgments xi

Chapter 1   The Ride 1
Chapter 2   It's Time for Some Answers 11
Chapter 3   All is in Divine Order 21
Chapter 4   Happy 50th. 31
Chapter 5   Getting Down to Business. 41
Chapter 6   P.I.N.. 49
Chapter 7   Take a Good Look in the Mirror 55
Chapter 8   I Want to Know my Mask. 63
Chapter 9   Love Spelled Backwards. 77
Chapter 10   In my Quiet World 85
Chapter 11   The Difference Between Surviving and Thriving 93
Chapter 12   It's Time to Make a Decision. 117
Chapter 13   This Time it's for Real 135
Chapter 14   Time to Heal. 145
Chapter 15   Smiling at My Zucchini 163
Chapter 16   An Unimaginable Invitation 177
Chapter 17   Oh Say Can You Sing 193
Chapter 18   Ride Millie Ride. 203

Epilogue. 211
Resources 215
Bibliography. 217

FOREWORD

By Bernie Siegel, MD
Author of *Love, Medicine and Miracles*

Denise's book shares the truth about healing one's life and how the body responds to the healing and the love of one's life and body. Her life is an example of survival behavior bringing together her mind, body and spirit through her action, wisdom and devotion.

Self induced healing is not an accident or a matter of good fortune; it is derived from the work of the individual. Solzhenitsyn describes it as a rainbow colored butterfly in his book *Cancer Ward*.

Denise shows us through her words and deeds how to create order, the rainbow, and transform your life, the butterfly. And when you create your new self, your body knows you are now loving your life, and it responds and does all it can to restore your health and keep you alive.

Reading this book can be a guide for anyone facing one of life's difficulties. If you have the courage and are willing to show up for practice and not fear change and failure, then let this book become your coach, and guide you to a healed life.

ACKNOWLEDGMENTS

This book would not have been possible without the generosity, love and commitment of the following extraordinary people in my life: Patricia (Pat) Moore, Mary Margaret Daughtridge, M. Brooks Solewater, Cindy Blazuk, and my niece, Kelly Anne McMullin.

Thank you to each and every person who believed I could, and would, actually write this book.

- ONE -

The Ride

"Individual commitment to a group effort – that is what makes a team work, a company work, a society work, a civilization work."

– Vince Lombardi

August 6, 2005 was the first day of the rest of my life.

At 4 a.m. my alarm clock clicked on with Ole Blue Eyes himself serenading me. While the sun still lay below the horizon, I navigated my way through the darkness toward the radio. Before I hit the off button, I took a few dance steps. With outstretched arms, pretending to be a bird, I sang along to "Fly me to the moon, Let me play among the stars. Let me see what spring is like on Jupiter and Mars."

Singing was one of the simple pleasures in my life. I had always had a song in my heart that would find its way to my lips. I was thrilled to begin the day with a song, especially this one. So much excitement bubbled inside me, I felt as if I *could* actually have flown to the moon.

Today was the day I had been training for over the past seven months. Along with over 4,000 other riders, I would ride the 2005 Pan Mass Challenge.

The PMC, as it is affectionately called by Bostonians, is a 192 mile bicycle ride through Massachusetts. The largest athletic fund raiser in the country, it raises millions of dollars annually for cancer research. Billy Starr founded the PMC in 1980 as a tribute to his mother, after she lost her life to cancer.

Donations that year totaled $10,200. This year 4,000 riders would pedal toward a goal of $23 million. The starting line at Babson College in Wellesley would see 2,500 through the gates. The other 1,500 would begin in Sturbridge, and we will all merge a few miles before the lunch stop. I was overjoyed knowing that, in some small way, I was making a difference.

Eager as I was to start, I was also tired. Training had started back in February with indoor spin classes. My almost 50-year-old body was complaining about the wear of the many miles I had pedaled over these past seven months. Calculating the miles of training between spin classes and actual time on the road with Millie (my bike's name, a nod to her birthplace: Milano, Italy) I estimated I had already cycled close to 2,000 miles.

In addition, I had been vexed by an earache, swollen gland, and a sore throat that had hung around for months. I had told my doctor about my physical discomfort but he assured me I was fine. Ignoring my inner voice's disagreement, I trusted what he told me. I didn't pursue the issue because the truth of the matter was, I wanted the expert to be right. Between working full-time as a sales executive for a demanding technology company, training for the ride, and my full social calendar, I had no space in my hectic life for illness.

Despite my fatigue, I had personally raised over $3,000 in donations. Fortunately I had committed to ride only the first day of the two-day ride -- 87 miles from Babson College in Wellesley, to The Massachusetts Maritime Academy in Bourne, at the neck of Cape Cod.

I knew I could make it because on back roads winding through small towns, I would be nourished in both spirit and body by the cheers of many spectators. Streets would be adorned with posters, balloons, water stations, and most importantly, smiling people with shouts of encouragement. Many of the wonderful supporters had either been cancer patients themselves or caregivers to loved ones who were afflicted with cancer.

At 5 a.m. Marsha, with Rose, Mim, and Pam, the longtime friends who would drive the "follow car," pulled up in front of my apartment. Marsha, my best friend of thirty years, would be riding with me this year. I was euphoric that Marsha and I would share this experience. Marsha is the type of person you want in your fox hole. She is a loyal and honest friend.

Marsha and I met thirty years ago. Both being born under the same sun sign of Virgo, we understood each other immediately. My birthday is September 10th and Marsha's is September 11th. In the earlier days of our relationship, having back to back birthdays was a call to duty to party for forty eight hours straight!

Marsha is one year younger, and I constantly remind her to respect her elders while she relentlessly teases me that I will always be older. I had never had a friend quite like Marsha. Her first encounter with my family was one April afternoon in 1977 when she came to my home for lunch. Marsha at that time was a skinny and distinctive twenty one year old, with a mane of crazy red, curly hair that was a clear indication of her unwillingness to conform. Wearing a long hippy flowing skirt, Frye boots, and a tattered and worn brown leather biker jacket, she entered my mother's world (the kitchen), and much to my surprise, Mama liked her.

Although my mother never admitted it, I think she thought Marsha was cool. In addition, since Marsha was too skinny, I think mama saw Marsha as a project. Her goal in life was to make sure all were well fed and...plump.

Over these past thirty years my friendship with Marsha has grown from a friendship into a sisterhood. All of my family considers her to be "one of us." In fact, when my mother was alive, Marsha was one of chosen few who were allowed to assist Lil (Mama) in the kitchen. So long as she cinched her wild red mane back while cooking, Marsha was allowed in.

The "Road Angels," as we tagged Rose, Mim and Pam, helped Marsha and me pack the car, and hoisted the bikes onto the rack at the back of the car. We drove Marsha's new Lexus along the dark and empty highway to the PMC starting line at Babson College.

Nearing the campus, I felt the energy of the crowd pulsing through my body. My heart was pounding. By the look on the other rider's faces, it appeared their hearts were beating as fast as mine. Exchanging glances, everyone's eyes had that silky look: a look of oneness, commitment, and deep regard for each other's wellbeing. These moments were ineffable so we trusted our eyes to tell the story.

As we approached the sea of bikes, the posted signs pointed us in the proper direction. The fastest riders, 15-18 miles per hour, filled in the front section. The next section was for riders who paced themselves at 12-15 miles per hour. This was the place where Marsha and I belonged, so we slid in and found our perfect spot. Nearing departure time, we momentarily abandoned our bikes and collected our farewell hugs and kisses from "The Road Angels." We confirmed our next meeting would be at the lunch stop. Squeezing between handle bars and peddles, and doing our best to avoid recently greased chains, Marsha and I navigated our way through the crowd back to our bikes. Millie was tuned up, sparkly and ready for the trek. Much to my dismay, Marsha had refused to baptize her bike, so we just referred to it as "Marsha's bike."

The Boston Red Sox Organization is the presenting sponsor for the PMC. Several of the executives shared a few moments with us from the platform. Choking back tears, I absorbed every note of the National Anthem sung by a young man named Rob. Rob was a local fire fighter, and he and his wife were PMC volunteers. Then the moment arrived to depart.

Filing in an orderly mass of titanium and carbon under the thirty foot high arch of yellow and purple balloons we began our trek. U2's "It's A Beautiful Day" played vociferously as 2,500 cyclists in a sea of color rolled on, bike-dancing to the tunes. Twenty minutes later once the crowd had thinned, Marsha and I clipped our bike shoes into our pedals and began full peddle strokes.

Keeping true to my ritual when I begin most journeys, I mumbled the Prayer of Protection.

> The light of God surrounds me,
> The love of God enfolds me,
> The power of God protects me,
> And the presence of God watches over me,
> Where ever I am, God is and all is well.
> So be it. So it is. Amen.

The Prayer of Protection is my automatic default prayer and passes my lips at least three times each day. James Dillet Freeman, the author of this prayer, became known to the world when this prayer was taken to the moon in 1969 by Buzz Aldrin on the Apollo 11 mission. Today I was taking it 87 miles to Bourne, not only for myself but for each and every PMC participant and all volunteers.

At a decent clip of fifteen miles per hour we took our time cycling these beautiful, back country roads. As I set the lead pace, every twenty minutes or so, I would ask "You with me?" and Marsha would quickly respond with a resounding "You got it, Mona." (Marsha's pet name for me).

Forty miles into the ride, we hit our stride. Me in the lead, and Marsha riding my draft a foot behind. We were in rhythm. Soon we would merge with the other 1,500 riders who had begun a few hours before us in Sturbridge, MA. God bless these folks. They were the two-day riders who, in addition to the physical commitment of riding the entire 192 miles, had stepped up to a financial commitment that exceeded the $2,600 each of the one day riders was required to raise.

As we approached the merge, I called out again, "You with me?" Marsha confirmed. Uniting as one solid mass of riders was pretty dicey. We had to dodge cars to our left; we had to watch for riders coming along side us on our right, and then we had to tackle a pretty steep hill.

Half way up the hill my muscles were burning and I was sweating profusely. As we climbed this long steep hill, the heat of the day reached its pinnacle, and the temperature had climbed to over 90 degrees. I attacked this hill with fierce determination because having to stop and start again in the middle of this steep hill would have been painful.

Checking on Marsha I called out again. This time I heard nothing. The coach in me surfaced immediately. I yelled to Marsha, "You got this hill, you got it Marsha, you got it!" Above the cacophony of automobiles, riders and bikes, my voice finally reached her and she followed my voice to the top of the hill.

Marsha's foot had slipped out of her toe clip and she whacked her shin on the clip itself. Lord only knows how that woman found the strength to clip in so quickly. With her shin bleeding, from a dead stop midway she rode the rest of the way up the hill while I awaited her arrival at the top. As she approached me with tears in her eyes and a grin on her face, she assured me her leg was fine. Not wanting to take the time now, she said we would tend to her wound at the upcoming lunch break. We took a moment for a supportive hug, a chuckle reaffirmed our commitment or lunacy, and then we re-joined the pack of riders.

As we approached the lunch stop, I knew that just around the corner lay the most challenging of the ride's 87 miles. Marsha, a novice, had no idea what she was about to witness. On display for the next mile were life-sized posters of the Jimmy Fund Kids, our reason for riding. There were kids with absolutely no hair smiling huge smiles and faces filled with the light of God. As I rode past these beautiful photos I offered a silent prayer of gratitude for the perfect health of the eighteen little ones in my life and tears welled up in my eyes. Marsha began to cry too. "I don't think I can do this Mona," she sobbed. It was tricky trying to ride and cry.

"We can do it," I promised. I reached out my hand to her, "Just stay next to me and look forward. They are our reason for doing what we're doing." Affirming that we *were* making a difference, locked hand to hand, we rolled slowly into the lunch stop.

Our three "Road Angels" met us with every necessity except for the one thing my stomach desperately needed: an antacid. So long as I was pedaling I had felt okay, but the minute I stopped for lunch the pains rose up like some monster from deep within my abdomen. I was in agonizing pain and did not want to admit it to anyone, including myself. My determination to finish the ride overrode any and all rational thinking. During the 30 minute lunch break I frantically headed toward the medical tent and guzzled ten shots of Mylanta. My stomach calmed down just enough for me to head back out on the road.

The 47 miles to the finish line were a blur. Marsha and I made a few quick water stops only to refill our camelback water sacks. The last water stop was eight short miles from the finish line. Determined to cross that line, Marsha and I ignored how sick I felt, and rolled on.

The "Road Angels" cheered us on as we cruised across. I was happy to be finished, and thrilled to see that the "Road Angels" had found a parking space right next to the finish line.

As Marsha and Mim loaded the bikes, I used every ounce of what little strength I had left to stay upright.

Because I was not much of a drinker, the faces of the "Road Angels" turned wide eyed, their eyebrows reaching to the sky as they were totally shocked when I announced, "Please take me to a liquor store."

My Dad's motto was always, "When you don't feel well drink blackberry brandy." He was right. The combination of my body temperature being elevated from the 87 miles on a hot August day, and the warmth of the brandy as it slid down my esophagus into my stomach temporarily relieved my discomfort.

But clearly there had to have been something drastically wrong for me to have consumed an entire pint of brandy in thirty minutes.

The end of the PMC ride was just shy of the Bourne Bridge, the gateway to Cape Cod. My sister, Deleta, lives five miles from that isthmus. Her house was our pre-planned final destination.

When I was born Deleta was 16 and the oldest of my four siblings, Carlo, Johnny, and Diane, followed at 13, 11, and 8, respectively. Dee was a great "big sister" to all of us and still is. Although she married when I was just five years old, she never drifted too far and always welcomed me into her newly budding family. She and Ed constantly took me along just as if I were one of their own. She is my confidant and my go-to person when I seek the truth, and very much like a mom when that's needed too.

Deleta is adroit. She also has a heart as big as Texas that you can feel the minute you are in her presence. I don't know of another woman who can spin a husband, six children, and ten grand-children, be the President of the Lady's Guild at church, and create unique gifts for all these kids, all the while making everyone feel like each is her priority. Deleta married Eddie McMullin when she was twenty years old. Fifty years later they are still a love story.

Ed is the quintessential Santa Claus. He is 6'1", and fills out his Santa suit quite well without padding. His long, snow-white hair and full beard, and clear blue eyes sparkle constantly and turn heads in any season. In the heat of the summer children abruptly stop breathlessly and stare at a living and breathing Santa sporting shorts and a tee shirt. With a twinkle in his eye, Ed quietly asks, "Are you being good?" and the kids without uttering a syllable furiously nod their heads in the affirmative. He is a great Santa, husband, father and grandfather, and a great cook.

My sister and Ed had prepared a sumptuous Italian feast for our arrival. The smell of meatballs and homemade gravy, (that's what Italians call spaghetti sauce) wafted thicker than the salt air. Their home is a true reflection of them: delightful, warm and comfortable. They are always the ultimate hosts.

The food smelled so good, but I was barely able to swallow a few bites. I felt as if someone had installed a shelf in my esophagus and nothing could get past it.

As we all settled in for the evening, I mustered up just enough energy to blow up my air mattress, set it up on the floor in the living room, and get myself ready for bed. I mumbled the prayer of protection, hoping for the miracle of a good night's rest. By morning my prayer had been answered. I was still tired, but I thanked God, Goddesses, and every deity available to thank, no remnants of the stomach monster remained.

The next day I was able to enjoy a few games of cribbage with Ed. He and I are fierce competitors at the board.

While we were playing, he noticed the swollen gland on the left side of my neck. He summoned Deleta to take a look. Astonished at the size of this gland she said, "What the heck is that?"

I told Dee and Ed that over the past two months I had called my doctor's office several times with concerns about the gland because it had grown to an abnormal size and it wasn't shrinking. And that the doctor had repeatedly assured me that it would take time for the gland to go down. According to my doctor there was no reason to see me. I just needed to be patient.

My sister issued me strict orders to hound the doctor until he examined my neck. I allayed her concern with a promise to see him as soon as I returned home.

Physically I felt taxed, but emotionally I was filled with a sense of great accomplishment for completing the ride. I had stayed true to my commitment to assist in the cure for cancer, this deadly disease which affects too many.

As usual, I departed beautiful Cape Cod defeated at the board, game after game.

Two

It's Time for Some Answers

*"Grief's worth more than the empire of this world
because it makes you call on God in secret.
The cries from those free of pain are cold and dull:
The cries of the agonized spring from ecstasy."*

- Rumi

I followed Deleta's orders and phoned my doctor, and once again he tried to dissuade me from an office visit as he was unsure of his availability. I stood firm on my promise to my sister. I was also fueled by my desire to feel better so I persisted.

"Well, if it will make you felt better, come in and I will take a look," he relented.

Hellooo… feel better???!!!! Isn't that what you are supposed to be doing? Helping people feel better?

The waiting room *was* packed but I wasn't leaving until I'd had at least a five minute examination. Eventually, I was led back to an examination room and a few minutes later my harried-looking doctor came in.

"All right, let's see what's going on here," he said as he extended his hands to both sides of my neck and pulled them away as if he had just touched hot coals. His face became ashen. He moved in reverse until he found himself supported by the counter about three feet behind.

It seemed to me, the walls began a slight motion inward, and for what felt like an eternity, he was silent. I waited for him to say something that would explain the color of his face.

The silence was broken by his apology. "I'm sorry. I should have seen you a month ago. A surgeon needs to look at that immediately so they can do a biopsy soon, preferably this week."

The walls moved even closer. Once I was finally able to formulate words, breathlessly I asked, "What could be going on? You said it was a swollen gland and it would return to its normal size. Sometimes swollen glands take a long time to retreat and I needed to be patient. Wasn't that what you've been telling me?"

"You might have lymphoma. I'm not sure but that doesn't look good and we need to get some answers sooner than later."

"Lymphoma? Do you mean cancer? I don't think so. There is no way I have cancer! You've been my doctor going on 14 years. Don't you think we would've realized it before now if I had some type of cancer?"

His blank stare bored a hole through my heart. Lord knows what that man was feeling. He had been a great doctor for me over these last several years. Clearly he was overworked, stressed, and inattentive to what needed attention.

With little else to say, I left his office and, on automatic pilot, headed to the front desk to complete necessary paperwork. The front desk staff would contact me with appointment options for a meeting with a local surgeon.

Alone in my car it seemed to take every last bit of energy just to slide the key into the ignition. I decided the best thing to do was to just get home, don't call anyone, say anything at this point, just get home.

I drove in silence, except for the thoughts that had my brain in a vice grip. Geez, could this really be lymphoma? I thought he might be overreacting a bit. I know I don't feel well but...Cancer? If I had cancer I imagined I would be feeling a lot worse than I did. I never thought I would ever have to hear those words coming at me.

When I returned home, I sat in my favorite chair and began to journal. Often, journaling had been my closest spiritual friend and a source of deep comfort.

Inside the pages of my journals I was able to retreat and bare my soul. Writing allowed me to sweep out cobwebs and dust off storage shelves in my mind, where I had sometimes collected unnecessary objects of doubt, self pity, and unworthiness.

After a few hours I called my sister Deleta and told her what the doctor had said. She and I both agreed he was most likely overreacting but it would be wise to have the biopsy.

The next morning the staff from my doctor's office called with a date near the end of August for the biopsy at Anna Jacques Hospital in Newburyport.

Prior to the biopsy I met with the surgeon for a preliminary examination. Marsha accompanied me. We checked in and waited for his arrival in a small cramped examination room.

Dr. Bentley was a talkative sort. As he spoke the corners of his mouth were just slightly turned up, a bit like a smile you see on a Buddha statue. He sat opposite me and leaned in and said, "I see this type of swelling all the time. Nine times out of ten it's just a nasty node that doesn't have the courtesy to return to its normal size on its own, so we have to help it."

His description of the procedure seemed pretty benign and not overly invasive. He went on to say, "I'll make a small incision, approximately two inches long in the crease of your neck and take a piece of the node for testing."

His near promise to me that he saw this all the time and his seeming lack of concern alleviated some of my fear, and supported my theory that my primary care physician might have been overreacting. I left his office reassured, and he said he would see me in a few days at the hospital.

I hoped the biopsy would be benign, but should the results show that I did in fact have cancer, I was pleased I had spent the last several years developing my knowledge and application of alternative healing therapies. I held certifications in Reiki, reflexology, polarity therapy, and sound healing. At a friend's suggestion, I decided to also investigate the healing work of Tom Tam. Tom was offering a one-day Tong Ren workshop the day before my scheduled surgery.

Tom Tam is a writer, poet, and healer, born in Tai Shan, China. Since 1982, he has been practicing acupuncture and Tong Ren healing with great success.

Tong Ren is a form of energy therapy for restoring health and vitality. It is based on a belief that disease is related to interruptions, or blockages, in the body's natural flow.

In a typical therapy session, the Tong Ren practitioner uses a small human anatomical model as an energetic representation of the patient, tapping on targeted points on the model with a lightweight magnetic hammer. The practitioner directs chi to blockage points corresponding to the patient's condition, breaking down resistance at these points.

The day of the workshop there were 50 participants. We had gathered on the top floor of an old barn on the rocky coast of Maine.

The information Tom shared was complex. Much of his work focused on the brain and the theory that the lack of circulation to the brain contributes greatly to disease. My head pounded from trying to grasp the breadth of all that information. My intention for attending was to meet him and ask for his opinion about the lump on my neck.

In the afternoon session he invited me into the center of the healing circle. Several people had small human anatomical models and a magnetic hammer. Tom instructed me to close my eyes and breathe deeply. As he called out, "solar plexus, neck, back of the head," I heard the gentle tapping sound the hammer made as each person tapped the area on their model.

As the volume of the tapping increased so did my temperature. I felt flushed and warm. The tingling and heat then moved to the swollen gland on the left side of my neck where I felt pulsing. By the end of that ten minute session the gland was half the size. I was thrilled and ready to forego the morning surgery. Tom was convinced I would benefit from his form of therapy, but still encouraged me to follow through with the biopsy to determine if it was, in fact, cancer.

The next day's surgery was set for 1:30 pm. I was headed home from downtown around noon to wait for Marsha to drive me to the hospital. Suddenly, I had an urge to go to the health food store. I had no reason to go, but the impulse was too strong to deny.

In the rear of the Natural Grocer, nearing the case with all the delicious looking prepared foods, I rounded the corner and exchanged pleasantries with a stranger. When she turned her head I noticed a bandage of significant size on the left side of her neck. My head spun a tad, wondering if that woman really was standing in front of me or if I had imagined her. Was I looking into the future?

As both of us left the rear of the store simultaneously, I was compelled to ask, "Would you mind if I ask the reason for your bandage?"

The woman responded, "Oh, I had a lump removed from my neck. My doctor thought I had cancer but I don't. I had Lyme disease and it got infected."

I turned my head to expose the lump on the left side of my own neck and asked, "Did it look like this?"

Her immediate response, "Oh wow…yes…it looked exactly like that."

I told her I was on my way to Anna Jacques Hospital for a biopsy. As I left the store she volunteered, "Hey, I know you are going to be fine, you are such a picture of health, but here's my name and number in case you need anything. I have a great team of oncologists at Massachusetts Eye and Ear in Boston."

Just the mention of the word, "oncologist" scared me. I emotionally dismissed her offer immediately, but when she handed me the piece of paper I tucked it in my pocket and headed off to meet Marsha.

Once we were at the hospital, remembering the surgeon's words, *he sees this all the time*, I was pretty calm. The preparatory routine for surgery began; lots of paperwork, questions, and reassurances. The nurses told Marsha I ought to be ready to leave in a few hours and that they would call her cell phone when it was time for her to pick me up.

The surgery room was small and sterile, with a few people sorting instruments and examining monitors. The anesthesiologist administered a little bug juice for me to relax, and the doctor offered a preliminary chat. He reassured me the procedure would take no longer than 45 minutes and he would visit me in recovery.

Through the intravenous needle came some type of sedative which relaxed me so much I was numb to the fact they were about to cut into my neck.

Unaware of how much time had passed, I sensed a commotion around me. I heard the word pathology repeated over and over again. The doctor was being very loud, yelling and barking orders at his staff. Everyone around me seemed to be moving at rapid fire speed and looking inquisitively at the surgeon. But I was unsure of exactly what was happening as I kept fading in and out of consciousness.

Then all of a sudden the room became still. It was just the doctor and me. He stepped to the side of the bed and said, "I need to tell you something, and you are not going to like what I have to say."

I didn't know at the time that I could have requested he refrain from sharing information until someone I knew and trusted was by my side.

Still foggy from the medication I was vulnerable to his next sentence. "You have cancer. You have a very serious, fast moving cancer and you need to do something about this immediately."

"Do I have lymphoma?" I asked.

He looked directly into my eyes and said, "I wish I *could* tell you that you have lymphoma. What you have is much more serious. It's called squamous cell carcinoma."

Jesus please help me. I thought this guy was pretty darn clear that he sees this all the time and not to worry.

After dropping that Napalm bomb, he departed. I was totally alone.

My life as I knew it would never be the same. Never, ever, ever. Nothing in my life would ever be the same. I had no idea what this all meant.

My mind raced with thoughts of everything I ever wanted to but didn't do. Questions of how much time I had now. How would I share the devastating news with all those I loved so dearly?

Above all, my mind circled round and round the thought, *How did this happen?* I was a health nut. I had just ridden 87 miles on my bike in one day. I swam three days a week. I walked an average of ten miles each week. I lifted weights and worked out at the gym as often as I could. Sure…maybe I ate a few too many strands of red licorice with red dye #3 in it, and dessert always, and maybe I didn't get enough sleep, but by all measures I was considered a health nut. This diagnosis was some kind of mistake but surely not one I had made.

Eventually a nurse appeared and momentarily rescued me from my mental gymnastics. She wheeled me into recovery where I was encouraged to sit up and eat something. The call to Marsha had been placed but nothing was said to her over the telephone. Marsha told me later that three nurses had met her in the lobby. By the looks on their faces they did not need to say a thing. She knew the news was not positive.

Marsha later told me that she had melted into a puddle of tears. And the nurses shared the urgency with her and reiterated that I would need to get into a good Boston hospital immediately.

In the recovery room, I waited for Marsha and wondered what could be delaying her. When she arrived, she had been crying and did not want me to see her upset.

We embraced and I comforted her by sharing with her what I knew to be true. That we would survive this life altering situation in much the same way we had meandered our way through the past 30 years. It was much easier to comfort her than it was to comfort myself. I would distract myself by extending comfort to others because at that point, I had no idea how to reconcile the news within myself.

About the time Marsha and the nurse got me settled into the car, Marsha's cell phone rang. On the other end of the call was my very nervous and emotional sister, Deleta. I overheard their conversation.

Deleta said, "I called back as quickly as I could. I'm at the Christmas Tree Shop buying all the decorations for Denise's 50th birthday party. Quick, tell me what's wrong"

Marsha answered "It's not good news Dee. It's not good at all." Marsha recounted everything she had learned from the nurses. She repeated the most important piece of information. "We need to get her to Boston as soon as possible. She needs to see a Boston doctor. Who do we know that could get her into see a good doctor in Boston?"

Marsha then handed the phone to me. The sound of my sister's voice felt like a warm blanket was being energetically wrapped around me. I knew she must have felt like someone just whacked her in the head a few times with a two by four. We talked only a few moments. Just long enough for her to tell me she loved me and that I would be fine. I asked Dee to call my sister Diane, and my brothers, Johnny, and Carlo, to tell them the news. I didn't have the physical or the emotional strength to tell them myself.

I felt reassured by Deleta's words that she and Eddie would be with me by noon the next day and that I would be soothed in the comfort of my sister's arms.

Later, Deleta told me that on the bench outside the Christmas Tree Shop, she collapsed and sobbed at the thought of possibly losing her baby sister.

For now, Marsha and I drove slowly to the beach to be with the "Road Angels" and the rest of our crew. Fifteen of us have comprised our unique version of a YaYa Sisterhood for about 20 years.

A few of the members rented a beach house for two weeks. The house was absolutely beautiful with a huge wraparound porch that overlooked the ocean. Each evening we were all invited to gather. There were many great cooks among us, so we took turns and created delicious feasts for the sisterhood. We all loved to eat and we loved sharing the dear affection we had for one another.

On our way there, Marsha phoned ahead, to report the results of today's surgery. There was silence on the other end of the telephone. Upon our arrival the normal raucous laughter was subdued. Vulnerability had permeated the entire house and I could tell by the looks on their faces everyone was holding back tears.

That cool summer evening had a chill that none of us could shake. While I rested on the couch, the sisterhood one by one gently caressed my head with soft kisses and a gentle touch.

With nothing left to say, I decided it was time to go home. I refused several offers for company that evening. I needed the tranquility of silence. I was exhausted. I wanted to lay my head down, pray, and sleep.

It took a while for that evening's good bye hugs and kisses as each person held on just a little bit tighter, and a little bit longer than usual.

Mim, who had been devastated by the phone call and had left the house, now walked headlong into my departure. Without a word, I opened my arms and she buried her face in my neck and sobbed. I reassured her all would turn out okay and I was up to the task.

Then Marsha and I drove the seven miles home in silence.

THREE

All is in Divine Order

*"There are two ways to live: You can live as if nothing is a
miracle; or you can live as if everything is a miracle."*

- Albert Einstein

Sleep didn't come easy. I tossed and turned while I wrestled with relentless thoughts of anxiety, fear, and sadness. When dawn finally arrived, I reached for the piece of paper with the woman's contact information from the health food store. Our meeting one another had not been by chance. My next step had already been revealed before I even knew I needed it. I had sensed she was the angel, sent by divine intervention, who was going to lead me into the hands of the medical team I now so desperately needed. I was anxious to dial her number, but telephoning a stranger this early in the day seemed too personal.

Because of my strong meditation practice, I was aware of the calming power of connecting to my breath, so while I waited to call her, I focused on slowing my breathing to help me remain calm.

At that moment the telephone beside me rang. It was my dear friend Paula. She called to see how I was holding up. News of my biopsy had traveled fast and Paula wasted no time in calling. Paula and I met ten years ago at our church, Unity on The River.

Unity is a spiritual community that welcomes and honors all paths to God. It is a positive and practical philosophy that promotes a way of life that leads to health, prosperity, happiness and peace of mind. I was thankful I had a spiritual community like Unity on The River. I was also thankful I had built a strong spiritual foundation. And it was rocked.

Paula is a beautiful, dark-haired Italian woman with chestnut eyes and wavy dark hair. She is an artist in every sense of the word, from the poetic way in which she speaks, to the clothes she wears, layering her garments upon her body just as she layers paint on a canvas.

Five years prior I had studied the depths of "spiritual and abstract" art with Paula. That was the first time I had ever laid paint on a canvas. It had helped me to uncover my inner Goddess. The elegance and exquisiteness of expressing my creativity through that medium had been and still was a great vehicle that had helped me to escape from my head and create from my heart: a feeling place, not a thinking place.

Our relationship was one of creativity, prayer, laughter, and lots of hugs.

After a silence between us that was thick with emotion, Paula asked me if I would like to pray and of course I said yes.

Before she began the prayer, Paula softly whispered, "You didn't do anything wrong."

Her tender words spoke to my wounded heart and I began to sob. On some level I knew what Paula had said was true, but I sure felt like I had done something wrong.

Too often we are scolded, not only as children, but as adults for doing something "wrong." I loathed the word "wrong." My spirit loathed the word, "wrong."

We really never do anything wrong. There is no wrong. There just *is* what *is*. No matter what I might have done in the past, when I chose to do what I did, it seemed like a good idea at the time. I had matured enough spiritually to know I created my own reality by what and how I thought, but since I never consciously chose this, I must have done *something* wrong. It wasn't deliberate.

This situation grabbed me by the neck and rattled me to my core. My ego wanted to play with my head and destroy my spirit. My humanness flooded in and the voice of Spirit was forced out. An acronym for EGO is Edging God Out. I got sucked into Edging God Out.

Eckhart Tolle says in his book, *A New Earth*: *The voice of the ego continuously disrupts the body's natural state of well-being. Almost every human body is under a great deal of strain and stress, not because it is threatened by some external factor but from within the mind. The body has an ego attached to it, and it cannot help but respond to all the dysfunctional thought patterns that make up the ego. Thus, a stream of negative emotion accompanies the stream of incessant and compulsive thinking.*

I was an incessant and compulsive thinker.

I wasn't able to fully digest her message at that time but Paula's reassurance, "You didn't do anything wrong" eventually opened me to the process of finally looking at my clandestine guilt.

I didn't know it then but instead of beating myself up, I needed my spirituality to forgive my personality and allow for my human-ness.

Then it was time for Paula and me to pray, time to trust the process and time to thank my ego for sharing. Centered prayers from the place of knowing that all is in divine order flowed through Paula and me; that place that knows only good, only love, only wholeness and only peace, oneness and light.

I told Paula about the woman at the health food store and that I was anxious to call her.

Paula said, "I hope she is someone who can help. I'll talk to you soon."

At eight o'clock. I dialed the number on the piece of paper and Alice answered the phone. "Hello Alice?"

"Yes."

"My name is Denise DeSimone; I met you yesterday at the health…"

Before I could finish my opening sentence Alice said, "I have been thinking about you since we met yesterday. How did it go?"

I took a deep breath, paused and said, "It didn't turn out so well. I need to see an oncologist and I wonder if you could tell me a bit more about your doctor in Boston."

Alice was not only willing to share her medical reference, she was also generous with her time, because from her own experience she knew what I was going through. She spent the better part of an hour on the phone with me.

The team of doctors she recommended at Massachusetts Eye and Ear Infirmary were the premier physicians in the field of head and neck oncology. People from all over the world seek treatment from these teams. Should I encounter any delays in setting an appointment, Alice offered to help.

The word oncology didn't freak me out quite as much that day as it did the day before because now it had a they-can-save-my-life kind of ring to it.

There is nothing quite like a cancer diagnosis to help prioritize your life. Things that seemed so critical just yesterday; like my daily routine, going to church, making sure I was well put together before heading out the door, and eating all the right things, now paled in comparison. But I needed to begin this day as normally as possible, so I took myself for a walk to help clear my head before making that emotional phone call to the Boston doctors.

For the next few days, I was in slow motion. I did not have the emotional energy to move forward at my normal rapid fire speed. Yet, at the same time, I couldn't devour life fast enough. To say I was devastated was an understatement. What could possibly be the reason for being served a death sentence?

I felt exposed in an unfamiliar way, turned inside out, tender and immobilized by it all. My eyes were constantly misty, not just because I was sad, but because life was so precious and may be cut short. Looking deeply into the eyes of those I loved I wondered if those moments were some of the last moments we would share. I was vulnerable. Vulnerability was the only "ability" I possessed.

I wanted to reach out *through* my vulnerability to my family, my friends and my spiritual community and invite them into my process. I needed their love and support. I didn't want to go through this challenging time alone. Being single and having no children left space for me to create my family of choice.

For several years I had been emailing daily messages of inspiration to a handful of friends and family. I called this "The Daily Dose." What had started with just a few people had now grown to nearly 60 recipients. This was the perfect vehicle for sharing my sad news.

"The Daily Dose"
September 5, 2005

Dear friends,

I had to go in for surgery to remove a few swollen lymph nodes that didn't have the courtesy to return to their normal size on their own. Well, things turned out a bit differently than we thought they would. Some nasty little cells found their way into my space and now we need to help them find their way out.

I am fortunate in that I have an appointment to see one of the best doctors and his team at Mass Eye and Ear in Boston. Next Thursday I will talk with these folks and set a plan of action into place. The next few days/weeks/hopefully not months might be a bit challenging to me and my request is that you keep the high watch for me.

Love is a painkiller and you are all filled with such love that I just know I will be fine and any pain will be at a minimum. Together we can move mountains so...I know we can usher these cells on their way. There may be times when the Daily Dose will have some gaps and at those times know that God and I are doing all we can to return to sending out the Daily Dose. One of my most precious moments of each day, is connecting with each of you.

Healthfully yours,

Denise

Almost immediately, my inbox was busy with well wishes and heartfelt concerns from the Daily Dose recipients. They comforted me and told me they would keep me at the top of their prayer list.

The bitterness of this cancer diagnosis had been soothed by the sweetness of their love for me. Tremendous surges of love bathed me energetically to where I needed to manage it. Managing love's tidal waves, I pictured those tiny, red, Valentine's Day candied hearts, as they melted into my being. Each one saturated one cell at a time, filling me with light and love, until my entire body was warm from the imaginary heat of these liquefied hearts. This exercise had helped me use their love in a tangible way.

Before I was diagnosed, I had doubted the love of my family and friends. On the surface, sure, I knew I was loved. However, my deeper self, the wounded self, felt unloved.

Clearly, I was loved. Family and friends poured their love all over me in so many ways. There was something to loving myself that had to do with healing myself. This was an area that was going to require deeper insight. It took me a while to realize it was the lack of self-love that had been the missing link.

I needed the catharsis of journaling. I transferred thoughts to words. I allowed my unedited feelings to flow from my heart and onto the paper. I felt the freedom to oust my emotions, to let them spill over onto the pages as I released the sadness from the depths of my being.

The new journal I had purchased specifically for this journey held such generosity in the quality of the paper. The pen would sink into the fiber just enough to return exactly what I needed to remain present to the process.

I had to trust the process and I *needed* to trust God. And, at the same time I knew I needed to allow for my human-ness. I needed to feel all of it.

Time to pray:

Dear God,

I know I am being held at this time. Together we will see me through this challenge with strength, gentleness and most of all love. I see my body strong and healthy, knowing there are more healthy cells than there are dis-eased. I will sing myself to wholeness, laugh myself to health and breathe myself into balance.

I am granted peace and joy and good health all these days moving toward my birthday and beyond. I am grateful in advance for the fun, laughter, kindness and my good strong dancing body during my 50th birthday celebration. I hold my family and friends in joy and love for this I am forever grateful.

***

When I went to see the oncologists in Boston to whom I had been referred, they said they did not have enough information and we needed further testing. I was happy the necessary tests were scheduled for after my birthday celebration.

It was time for another Daily Dose update.

Dear hearts,

Thank you all for your well wishes, prayers and love. Next week on Monday and Tuesday I will be in Mass Eye and Ear going through several tests. Friday I meet with a team of treatment doctors and set the stage for what will be the most difficult ride of my life.

On the physical plane this is a very serious situation and on the spiritual level this is an opportunity for us to hold the highest vibration we can muster. To say I am not scared would be a lie. I am very scared. And I will choose faith over fear. That being said, I am truly grounded in my faith, in my belief that all things are for a higher and greater purpose, more than anything...love always prevails.

I am so blessed with the people in my life. There are no words to describe the depths to which I feel this connection. In the face of all that is going on, I feel like I am the wealthiest woman on the planet. Because when it comes right down to it...all we really have is each other.

Thank you for holding me close. Love yourselves unconditionally. You are my medicine!

Love,
Denise

My sister Diane was one of the first to sign up for my daily inspirational emails. Her husband, Bill, of almost 40 years had been diagnosed with stage IV lung cancer a few months prior to my diagnosis. The seriousness of my condition layered on top of her husband's health challenge pressed her emotionally.

Diane is eight years my elder. As an infant I was her real live doll. Because both my parents held full-time jobs, she was my number one babysitter. During our childhood we suffered our sibling struggles. She was a wannabe hair stylist, so my Mom gave her carte blanche to practice on *my* head. For several years my bangs varied in length, as did the rest of my hair.

However, Diane was a talented dancer and studied dance for many years at Betty's Dance Studio in Newton Corner. Stuffed silently into the corner of that studio are some of my earliest memories of absolute boredom. Diane would continuously tap, tap, and tap around the house in her tutu outfits religiously practicing for her annual recital. Although she was the shortest in her dance troop, she was the best.

Everybody loves my sister. She is a fabulous supportive little league mom, attending every one of her boys' games and working the crowd with her great sense of humor. Although she is all of 4'11" her presence fills a room. Her smiling dark eyes and wide grin, with a slight space between her two front teeth, welcomes you into her fun world.

Diane is warm and kind, and at the same time is solid in her convictions and doesn't budge when she knows what she wants. Raising four boys prepared her for whatever life tossed her way. Living next to our parents made her their primary care giver, and Diane was a faithful daughter to the end.

After she received my Daily Dose update, as a loving-kind gesture, Diane distributed this email to the group.

I HAVE AN AMAZING SISTER!!

She's faced with one of the scariest situations that life could hit you with and she is as gracious as ever. This is a wonderful, moving message that she sent out today. No wonder she is loved by so many of us --- far and wide.

When she was born, I was eight years old and I was overjoyed. I had my own little live doll to play with and take care of. Of course, my mother thought she looked like a little monkey and threatened to "send her back to the Indians" (whatever that meant!) Actually she was adorable and Mama dressed her like a fashion plate. I remember her toddling around Deleta's (my oldest sibling) graduation party in a pink dress that stuck out straight from her waist with crinoline layers under it. I even think I have a photo of her that day.

She was my responsibility summers and after school and we spent an abundance of time together at Cabot Park and at home. She insists – to this day - - that I threatened to throw her out of our second story bedroom window when she was 5 or 6 yrs old because she was going to "tell Daddy you were kissing Billy at Cabot Park". I do not remember this --- but it sounds about right!

She is special to everyone but especially my children and grandchildren. Auntie Denise is the "fun Auntie" and she has somewhat adopted my children and grandchildren as her own and it's wonderful. What other auntie would bring my granddaughters Rachel and Abby rubber boots to go puddle jumping in -- and then join them! Or bring Abby her own gorgeous drum and attempt to teach her the art of drumming at the tender age of three!

Denise will get the strength she needs to get through these next few months from all of us. She is always there for everyone and we will all be there for her. To quote her message of earlier today, "I am so blessed with the people in my life; there are no words to describe the depths of which I feel this connection. In the face of all this I feel like the wealthiest woman on the planet. Because when it comes right down to it…all we really have is each other." How true! As she feels she is blessed with all of us in her life, we are certainly blessed with knowing and loving her.

An email tsunami flooded my inbox with an outpouring of affection from many considerate and loving souls. It felt like Christmas in September. My sister bestowed a gift upon me with her kind, sincere, and ardent words.

How could I have ever doubted the love of my friends and family? I truly *did* feel like the wealthiest woman on the planet.

So many people equate wealth with money. I realized I could have been more successful financially. I could have developed a more serious career and acquired huge assets. In the final analysis of my place in life, I *had* developed a career. I had developed a career out of loving people. These people were my markers for success. My wealth had nothing to do with money. It had *everything* to do with love, connection, and experience of the rich and raw healing power of love.

There's a Tim McGraw song about a man who receives a cancer diagnosis and a friend asks, "*So what did you do when they told you the bad news?*" The man's response; "*I went sky diving, I went Rocky Mountain climbing, I went 2.7 seconds on a bull named Fu Man Chu, and I loved deeper, and I spoke sweeter, and I gave forgiveness I'd been denying. Some day I hope you get the chance to live like you were dying.*"

I related to this at a visceral level.

Every cell of my being was permeated with gratitude for having been granted this opportunity to live like I was dying. I would walk around my house singing the words to that song so loudly, I was sure the mere vibration of my voice would shake the cancer loose.

The strange paradox; I would never ever wish a diagnosis of cancer on anyone, yet…at the same time… if only for one day, I wished others could participate in life at this level.

Four

Happy 50th

"Buon Compleano"

- Happy Birthday in Italian

I was truly blessed by the love of my family. They wove themselves like thread into a strong bolt of fabric that would bear the weight of the world, if needed. I placed myself into the family fabric knowing I would be held, supported, loved, and carried through my ordeal. This fabric was not only important for me; it was important and necessary for each of them, as they would need to carry each other through this as well. If I had not been blessed with them as my family, I would have absolutely corralled them into my inner circle of friends.

Our family tree is huge, its roots deep and branches expansive, embracing many. My maternal and paternal grandparents arrived in America in the late 1800's from the Province of Avellino, in the Campania Region of Italy. My father was one of 11 and my mother was one of 14 children. My siblings, two brothers and two sisters have raised 18 children. The majority of those eighteen are married, and have 31 children among them. Additionally, Seko a beautiful, bright-eyed, wide smil'n, little boy came to us from Ethiopia.

Although I adore kids, and spend most of my time with them when at family gatherings, I knew from an early age that having my own children was not in my future.

In a family photo you can see the resemblance we five siblings all have to our parents. We all top off with chestnut hair. Each of us has big brown eyes and was blessed with perfect smiles.

Our parents were staunch Catholics and the strength of family was a direct connection to the faith our parents instilled in each of us from an early age. I am grateful to them for having created this strong spiritual foundation.

We never drift too far from one another. The two generations of nieces and nephews are a tight knit group generally spending weekends together. The little ones are constantly back and forth begging their parents for sleepovers with their cousins. The measurement of how much fun they had is determined by how thoroughly exhausted they are when they return to their respective homes.

The thought of not being around to see these sweet little ones grow through life broke my heart.

Birthdays never go uncelebrated, and usually involve some type of creative activity for all to participate in.

Soon we would celebrate my 50th birthday. My siblings and some close friends had decided on a theme for my party. Clandestine meetings had taken place over the past months, and they kept the specifics from me.

The excitement of celebrating my big day permeated the air. I could almost smell Italian rum cake wafting through the air every time I thought about the party.

Of course the news of my cancer had filtered through the guest list, and the attendees were stunned. I didn't want the results of my biopsy to dilute the celebration, but I would be lying if I said thoughts that this might be my last birthday had not entered my mind.

These people were, for sure, my medicine, and I was going to drink a case of each of them over these next few weeks while I focused on celebrating my life and life itself.

Let the celebration begin!

I couldn't wait for my party. I wanted to look into the eyes of those I loved, hug them tightly, smell their different scents, notice the quirky ways their mouths move when they speak—all the things I might have taken for granted or let slip by unnoticed because of unimportant distractions.

In addition to my 50th celebration, I had planned a shamanic fire ceremony to mark my first 50 years, and the threshold I would cross as I entered into the next phase of my life.

The most auspicious time for this type of ceremony is on or around the time of one's birthday. These intimate gatherings take place around a blazing fire.

Marc is my shaman, my acting coach, and most importantly, my friend. This night he was the master of ceremonies.

Marc's six foot stature, his sparkling eyes, thick salt and pepper hair, contagious laugh, and prodigious personality make him someone people flock to. Whenever Marc would open his arms and scoop me up into one of his monstrous bear hugs, whispering in my ear that all is right with the world, a calm feeling would seep into my soul. That evening I was enormously grateful to him for supporting me and assisting me in helping to create my special evening as a right of passage.

Guests began to arrive at Marc's at the scheduled time of 7:00 PM, eager to participate in an ancient and sacred ceremony.

Birthdays are poignant because the cyclical energies of the universe are the same as when we were born. Astrologically the sun is aligned in much the same place as one's birth day. It is an auspicious time for deep renewal work.

Marc's expansive backyard was specially decorated. The weather Goddesses had brought us superb autumn weather. It was the proverbial clear fall evening, where the smell of summer lingered, and the evening wrapped itself around you like an exquisite shawl. The air was just cool enough that all the bugs were somewhere else. The stones shaping the circular fire pit resembled clusters of children piling on top of one another playing pig pile.

Marc's stirring the fire had fanned a spectacular partnership between shimmering embers and dancing flames. The fire was blazing and the energy was soft and supple. It was important for each guest to participate in the ceremony, including Deleta and Ed, who had never before experienced anything quite like this.

During the initial phase of the ceremony, Marc directed the group of twenty to separate into two groups. He then asked them to face each other leaving approximately three feet between them. This formed a pathway which represented the path of my life. Marc instructed me to walk the path slowly and deliberately. As I walked the path of my life each person blessed me with their words. Each and every person whispered something precious and meaningful to me.

Deleta stood near the end of the pathway, and as I passed, she whispered, "I am as happy today as I was 50 years ago on the day you were born." Her words solidified within me how important my life was to her. A stream of tears moistened my face.

These were good tears, salty tears, tears I used as a form of holy water as I blessed myself with them. I anointed my forehead, my lips, my eyes, and especially my throat and neck.

During a fire ceremony each participant faces the fire from the South because that is the direction where the energy of death, rebirth and transformation is, and it is the highest point for releasing and receiving. I was now standing before the fire ready to give and receive.

All guests followed me and circled the flames, creating a continuum, as Marc called in the four directions: North, the energy of the Buffalo which supports us spiritually while living in the physical world; East, the energy of the Eagle allowing us the beauty of illumination and inspiration; South, the energy of the Serpent representing death, rebirth, and transformation, and West, the energy of the Jaguar strengthening us on our journey.

I entered at the South and began to sing my song. A song without words, just the sounds from deep within my being. It was the song of my soul, the song of my heart, the song in my bones. The song of my journey. The song of my cancer that was sitting perched in my throat just waiting to be released from the imprisoned place it had been. Possibly for the past 50 years. The flood gates opened and I let go.

I sang and I chanted. I released all sounds that were waiting to be expressed. So deeply immersed in the moment I could hear the sound of my voice, but it was somehow unfamiliar to me. The sound was irrelevant. What mattered was what I *felt*. I felt as if Mother Earth had opened her womb, and from a safe and loving place had assisted me to give birth to a new me.

Drumming during fire ceremonies is one of my favorite activities. I let loose on the drum and let the heart beat of the Mother fill me to overflowing. The beat itself flowed down my arms and out my hands. To me, it's one of the most transcendent ways to connect with Spirit. Chanting and singing, I unleashed any self-imposed constraints, and I pounded the drum again and again, creating a dense African beat. Everyone began to sing and dance along. It was a visual and audible soul feast.

As the embers of the fire glowed against the dark night, and each of us prepared to leave, Deleta came to me and said, "What a wonderful evening, honey. I would not have missed this for anything. I love you. See you tomorrow."

Emily Dickinson says it best: *Forever is composed of nows.* Each and every moment of our lives is critically important. To enjoy, to be "in-joy" during these moments is our most important task. We never know our deadline on earth.

Our perception of illness as a culture has been distorted. Physical challenges are doorways: doorways of transformation. The fire ceremony had prepared *my* doorway of transformation. I was filled with appreciation that the people I loved were witnesses at my side. They not only supported my every step along the way, but also participated and owned it. It was one of the most glorious nights of my life.

***

My friend, Jean, escorted me to my 50th birthday party in her snazzy new black Audi. We made our way through Newburyport, and onto Plum Island. Plum Island, Massachusetts is a tourist attraction because of its stunning beaches.

She dropped me off at the door. As I placed my hand on the door to enter, my heartbeat was nearly audible.

Most of my family members and friends, who have been a part of my life anywhere from five to fifty years, awaited my arrival.

I decided to go casual so, I wore my favorite jeans, my favorite black cowboy boots, and a new lightweight red sweater, with small black buttons dressing the front and black piping on the edges of the collar, sleeves, and bottom. People would tell me all the time how great I looked in red. My olive skin and deep dark eyes glowed against the deep crimson.

I had removed the dressing on my neck, because I did not want birthday photos of me with bandages on my neck.

I was ready to boogie.

As I walked through the door, I smiled the biggest smile, and within moments felt the enormity of the love that filled the hall. In that moment reality hit me. The color of my face began to match my red sweater and I began to sob. This could be my last birthday. I feared that I might not have the fortitude to stay alive for all these loving people.

The first to reach me as I continued to sob were Toni and Hank, two dear friends I met in 1977. The three of us wove ourselves into a triangular bear hug, saying so much without uttering a sound.

My brother John was next in line. Johnny is the funny man of the family. He always has a joke to tell and commands an audience. The kids love Uncle Johnny because he bribes them with lots of money to do the simplest things like give him lots of kisses or sit on his lap forever and answer all his crazy questions. At family functions he gets the kids so riled up, and it's usually him we have to quiet down, not the kids.

He sold me my first car, a 67 VW Beetle. He handed me the keys and said, "Here's first gear, here's second, here's third, and here's fourth. This is reverse, and don't forget to push down when you need to backup. Have fun." That is when I was given the name "Rubber legs" by my friends. It took a while, but I mastered the art of the standard transmission.

As only my brother John can do, while crying and kissing me, then kissing me and crying, he kept stepping back to look deeply into my eyes. Holding me by my shoulders, he repeatedly told me, "You are going to be just fine you know. You will make it through this. I promise you will make it through this."

He knew what I was about to undertake because my sister-in-law Karen, his wife of 38 years, had been diagnosed with breast cancer three years earlier and had been through the rigors of chemo, radiation, and surgery after surgery. "Warrior Woman" was my name for Karen. She kept her priorities in order and defied every statistic the medical field threw at her. Now more than ever, she was my hero.

After my brother released me from his bear hug, Karen approached me.

We just hugged and she whispered, "I love you." She didn't need to say a word nor did I. Being with someone else who has cancer, you automatically communicate at a cellular level.

Karen is an amazing woman. She came into our family when I was only eight years old. When she and Johnny began dating she was in nursing school at a local hospital. She would come over after school and my mother would teach her how to cook while they made dinner for the family.

Karen loves to laugh. That's a good thing living with my brother. She is very Irish looking with light brown hair and hazel eyes that twinkle when she laughs. When her oldest son asked her advice about parenting, prior to the birth of his first son, she told him to show his son how much his father loves his mother, and everything will always work out.

One by one I wove my way around to each guest. For most of them this was the first time they were seeing me after hearing the news. Tears streamed down our faces. We could not hold on to each other long enough or tight enough. How they felt about losing me was apparent.

After lots of tearful hugs, I finally had a moment to look around and admire the décor. For so many years I had been threatening a trip to Italy. I guess it was something I had always planned to do but never quite got around to.

The first chance I got, I decided, I was going to Italy!

The decorating team had brought a bit of Italy inside the walls of the hall, and brought my dream to life. Each wall was adorned with the Italian flag. Centerpieces were wicker baskets filled with bread, a wooden cutting board and a knife. Bottles of red wine were everywhere. Table clothes were the colors of the Italian flag. An Italian caterer had the entire hall filled with the aroma of garlic.

Off in the corner was a table with one of my most favorite desserts in the whole world, Italian rum cake. The cake must have been three feet long by two feet wide, and four inches high. I suggested we begin dinner with dessert, but my sister Diane disagreed.

Dinner was fabulous! Several different flavors of pasta, meatballs, salad and vegetables, along with some other Italian treats. Marsha's favorite eggplant parm was the first thing on her plate.

Beer and wine flowed. This was just the way I wanted it, with everyone celebrating life, and enjoying every moment.

At the opposite end of the hall, was a huge screen and projector. My friend Mim had produced a retrospective of my life. She is a creative genius and I couldn't wait to see what was going to appear on the screen. Once dinner ended, Mim invited everyone to witness my first fifty years.

There were photos of me as a baby, a young child, photos of the ugly teenage years, trips taken with friends and family, silly photos, serious photos, group photos and photos of friends and family who had passed on. The show was complete with popcorn comments from the crowd, as they were moved to share thoughts about these snapshots of our lives.

During the hour, I traveled from the real to the surreal, wondering if I would be joining my friends and family that had passed on. I felt suspended above the crowd as I watched them celebrate my life. I drifted in and out of scenes from my own funeral; I was overcome with sadness which ignited a chain reaction. Tears burst forth from each of us.

"Now that we have celebrated your life up to here, let's see what comes next." That is what Diane said as she and Deleta handed me an envelope with a ribbon around it. Inside the envelope was a homemade gift certificate for an all expense paid trip to Italy for the three of us. If that proved to be my last birthday, there could not have been a better finale.

The first song the DJ spun was Gloria Gaynor's "I Will Survive."

The first few familiar notes of the song beckoned everyone to end their conversations and join in a resounding, "I Will Survive."

That song had become my mantra.

As we began to dance, everyone formed a circle around me. My sister Diane was the first to join me in the middle. One by one each guest took turns and shared a few precious moments in the middle of the circle with me.

Rumi says it best in his poem entitled "Love is the Cure."

> Love is the cure
> Your pain will keep giving birth to more pain
> Until your eyes constantly exhale love
> As effortlessly as your body yields its scent.

Every part of their bodies had exhaled love and I had inhaled every bit of it. Love would be the fuel I so needed over the next few days.

The gift certificate from my sisters was a tangible survival goal that I was determined to reach. I tucked it safely away in the front pocket of my jeans.

FIVE

Getting Down to Business

"Death pushed me to the edge. Nowhere to back off. And to the shame of my fears, I danced with abandon in its face. I never danced as free. And Death backed off, the way dark backs off a sudden burst of flame. Now there's nothing left, but to keep dancing. It is the way I would have chosen had I been born three times as brave."

- Mark Nepo

Founded in 1824, Massachusetts Eye & Ear Infirmary is an international leader in ophthalmology and otolaryngology research and a teaching partner of Harvard Medical School.

The hospital's 11th floor waiting room's all glass walls spanned a beautiful section of The Charles River. The sunny, warm, crisp September day had the river peppered with small Sunfish sailboats, amphibious Duck Tour boats that run on land and end up launching themselves into the river.

As I stared out the window, waiting to be called for an MRI—I loathed even the acronym MRI—I wished I was on any one of those sail boats instead of heading for a long, cramped, silver-lined tube whose clanging of magnets, like the mallet of an angry butcher, would pound in my ears for the better part of an hour.

Whenever that acronym came up in conversation, I had always declared, "You will *never* get me in one of those things. I am the most claustrophobic person on the planet. Bar none! I would rather die than be stuck in one of those machines." The reality is I did not want to die.

A sweet faced woman stood in the doorway of the waiting room and called my name. As we approached the MRI room, I prayed the Ativan I dissolved under my tongue an hour ago had kicked in.

Once inside the room, the technician laid me onto the gurney, protected my ears with a pair of what looked like Kotex pads, and asked me to scoot up a little. As I obliged, my head effortlessly slid into a cage and much to my surprise they lowered the other half of it over the front of my face and snapped it together. Immediately I knew I was not nearly as sedated as I needed to be.

"Please, let me out of this contraption" I said.

Obviously, the technician heard my heart beating from where she stood and hurried to unsnap the cage to release me. She asked, "Do you have any more anti-anxiety pills? If you do, I suggest you take another."

Concerned about causing a delay, I said, "That's a good idea but I hope this doesn't cause a glitch in your schedule."

She touched my arm and said, "Not to worry. We can wait as long as you need."

Deleta was holding the pills in her purse, so I returned to the waiting room and popped another under my tongue and waited for that sweet tiny pill to take effect.

Thirty minutes later there I was, back in the MRI, perfectly calm and ready to reunite with the tunnel of love, as long as Marsha could stay with me.

I asked the technician, "May my friend stay in here with me?"

She said, "Nobody can have any metal on or in their person when near an MRI machine." Turning to Marsha she asked, "Do you have any metal in your body from any surgeries?"

"No. All I have to do is remove my jewelry."

Marsha removed both her rings, her gold earrings, and belt and brought them to Deleta for safe keeping and returned to us.

I felt safe and comforted by Marsha's warm hand on my foot. Her proximity was also comforting. In the event I panicked, she would be able to slide me out of the machine immediately.

Even with my ears protected, the MRI was annoyingly loud. I turned the banging into a healing tune at a Native American Indian drumming circle.

After what seemed like only a few moments, I was released and was free to leave the hospital.

When it was all over, it was difficult for the other two members of the dream team to get Ativan-intoxicated, "rubber legs DeSimone" down the hall, onto the elevator, and into the car.

Every few feet I wanted to stop and sit on the floor in the hallway. The level of sedation it took for me to tolerate the MRI caused me to sleep the entire way home and all the way through to the next morning, only to awake and make the trip again.

The second day was the most important day of all. It was the day for exploratory surgery. This surgery would give us the answers we needed. Will they find the primary tumor? Where is it? What did the MRI show about how far the cancer had spread? What would be the window of time before I needed treatment? And, the most important question for me was, will I be able to delay treatment to pursue a more preferred, alternative approach?

Today, Ed had come along. Deleta needed her husband's support.

The waiting room was quiet. There really wasn't much to say. I attempted to calm my nerves by distracting myself trying to differentiate patient from caregiver. In their street clothes everyone in the room looked healthy. At first glance I couldn't tell which was which.

Finally a nurse called my name. I was escorted to my designated cubicle so I could complete my to-do list: undress, put on a Johnny (I wonder who named them that) then meet her in the office to answer what felt like a thousand questions. Next, I needed to meet with the anesthesiologist to calculate how much anesthesia they would need to administer to keep me under.

Once all duties were checked off, I returned to the waiting room sporting my new "snazzy" Johnny and matching skid proof footsies.

Another hour passed before my name was called again. This time it's real. Ed, Deleta, and Marsha each embraced me with soft but firm hugs that sent a reassuring message straight to my heart that everything is going to be okay.

I wanted to believe them, but my nerves had built a barrier between me and this truth. I could not let fear overtake me. I had to stay in the moment, and trust the doctors. And pray they find the primary tumor. I went to sleep with a proverbial lump in my throat, ironically, just about at the location in question.

I turned to join the nurse and we headed to the basement's operating room. No more "Dream Team" by my side.

Three hours later, I opened my eyes in recovery to see all three faces smiling down at me.

The first words that burst forth from my sister's mouth were, "They found the primary tumor; they found it!" Exactly the words I wanted to hear. I was still too sedated to express my excitement, but Deleta, Ed and Marsha more than compensated for my lack.

In the recovery room the nurses gave Deleta all the necessary paperwork including instructions on my care over the next week; a liquid diet only, lots of rest and I should keep my voice quiet. Quiet? It was apparent these nurses didn't know me.

"The doctor's office will be in touch to schedule our next appointment. It will most likely be within the week," said one of the nurses.

Two days later the oncology nurse telephoned to schedule the next appointment. Her instructions, "You need to be at Mass General Hospital's Yawkey Cancer Center day after tomorrow. Plan to be there for the entire day. You will be meeting with different teams of doctors throughout the day. They will review their findings and set the treatment protocol." She also encouraged us to have all of our questions written out.

It was an exhausting task to spend another entire day with the white coats, but it was the first of many long routine days on my journey toward healing.

On that day, the guest list included the heads of Head and Neck Oncology, Chemotherapy, and Radiation and their student minions.

The plethora of questions that kept burning a hole through me were, "Why did all this happen? How did I, a woman who is a health nut, obsessed with physical fitness, lifting weights, swimming every other day, walking 2-3 miles daily, cycling, golfing, nutritionally diligent, end up here?"

Over the past 10 years, I had studied alternative therapies and obtained certifications in Reiki, Reflexology, Polarity Therapy, and Sound Healing.

The fire for knowledge around alternative therapies had burned in me for a long time. I built a healing practice combining these modalities and, in addition to my full-time work, treated a few clients each week.

In addition, my study of various spiritual disciplines had shone a light on a path where I walked closely with God. I was stimulated by anything spiritual. I had assumed this multi-pronged, masterful combination, was a surefire plan to maintain a strong and healthy body. I guess I had been mistaken.

When we entered The Yawkey Cancer Center, I felt as if we had walked into a restricted area at NASA. Everyone wore a crisp white coat, stethoscopes draping their necks, with the ice cold metal disk at the end stuck in their left pocket for safe keeping. Faces were friendly, but the entire place had a certain seriousness about it. Everyone walked with intention and determination, weaving in and out of one another's path in order to get to their destination without delay.

The Dream Team boarded the elevator and ascended to the fifth floor. Surprisingly, we were quickly directed to follow the nurse down a long hallway into a tiny, cramped room with several pieces of equipment, a few chairs, and a sterile stainless steel sink. The room felt claustrophobic, with barely enough air for my sister Deleta, Marsha and me. I nervously waited for the doctors to deliver their reports.

I chose the most comfortable chair which happened to be a leather type recliner, assuming its comfort would help soothe my nerves. Now, my heart beat was a clarion… thump…thump…thump… pounding in my ears.

The first team that arrived was the surgeon who had performed the exploratory surgery and the chemotherapist. While looking at the surgeon's hands I had a bubble thought, *How the heck did those baseball mitt size hands of his find their way down my throat?* .

After all appropriate introductions, the medical team shot straight to the point. With very little emotion my surgeon said, "The diagnosis is stage IV cancer with the primary tumor on the back of your tongue where your tonsil used to be. The cancer has spread to both sides of your neck and it is traveling with excessive speed. The results indicate that we need to move quickly. If we don't get you into treatment soon you may not be alive for Christmas."

Christmas was only 90 days away.

It felt as if this cancer was some type of "alien" that had invaded my body, my temple, or as the Buddhist refer to it, my "skin bag." Given my knowledge of holistic treatments, I wanted to take a more alternative approach. But I didn't have the time.

Without so much as a glance in each other's direction, Deleta, Marsha and I listened to the proposed treatment protocol. Deleta wrote their every word so we would be able to later absorb what, at this point, were just words filling our ears. This was so scary it was impossible to take it all in.

These docs were as direct as an arrow's trajectory to a bull's eye. The information was explained in great detail. They didn't candy coat a thing. The head of the team asked, "Have you ever had a strep throat?"

I answered, "Yes, a few times, actually. I can handle it."

He said, "Okay, now multiply that by 100, and that's about the level of pain you should expect. The amount of radiation required to halt this cancer will burn the outside of your face and neck, and will damage the internal tissue of your mouth and throat."

His comment pretty much splattered me all over the room. He continued, "Unfortunately, you will not be able to eat for several months so we will surgically insert a G-tube into your stomach for nourishment."

"A what tube?" I asked. I quickly learned it is a nine inch feeding tube to be inserted just below my rib cage on the left-hand side of my body directly into my stomach. Three inches on one end is inserted into my stomach and the seven inch protrusion is capped at the opposite end and would be taped to my opposite side when not in use.

Before we departed Mass Eye and Ear, the doctors walked us through, step by step, what was coming: four rounds of chemotherapy, two months of daily radiation, with double treatments daily for the last two weeks.

As he explained the radiation procedure he made sure I understood everything that would be involved.

He said, "We will mold a very sturdy mask to your face that looks like fine fishnet stockings. It is crucial that during each treatment we keep you perfectly still to reduce any chance of potential movement. Movement of any kind may cause the radiation beams to destroy your spinal column.

The mask will be secured to a gurney and will cover your entire head, face, and neck, and will extend halfway down your chest."

I thought I had heard the worst of it until the doctor said, "The other potential aspect of this protocol is a radical neck dissection. This is a surgical procedure where the entire left side of your neck will be removed: your SCM (sternocleidomastoid) muscle, all the lymph nodes, your submandibular glands, and your jugular vein."

I knew their mouths were moving but I could not hear clearly. I felt as though I had been transported into a tank of water. Their voices slowed to where they were distorted. I made every attempt to maintain composure. I just kept nodding. My entire body was covered with perspiration. And I was as jittery as if I had just drunk a gallon of caffeine. The voice inside my head was screaming, "Nooo... Nooo....Nooo...remember me, the most claustrophobic woman in the world? How can you possibly think I will be able to emotionally or physically survive these treatments?"

The thick air suddenly felt even thicker making it harder and harder for me to breathe. I felt numb. This meeting was too much to comprehend. Do I really want to go through this torture? It was time to prioritize my life and process the information that I had been handed. I needed to make a decision whether to live or just let myself die.

Deleta, Marsha and I left the hospital and drove the fifty mile return trip home in deafening silence. As we approached my home, I informed the "Dream Team," "I needed to be alone.

The silence from the car carried into the solitude of my living room. For several hours I sat in total darkness aware of all the *stuff* that surrounded me.

The lights outside softly illuminated the items in my home as I looked around and realized, this *stuff* held no value for me. Not even my dearest friend, my $2,000 Larivee custom-made guitar, that had been such a loyal companion over the past 10 years. So often she had carried me away on the vibration of her perfect sound. During a time like this, she was the first place I would normally retreat, but not tonight.

The only items of importance were the many photographs that seemed to have wallpapered my refrigerator; visages of the little ones in my life celebrating special moments in their lives, my parents, siblings, friends with goofy smiling faces, and several photos of me looking like the happiest person alive. I stood for an hour in front of my refrigerator staring at their faces.

These people were my foundation. The importance of these relationships could not be overstated. Now, there was no question, these people loved me dearly. They too were all hurting from the news of my illness. I wanted to protect them from this hurt but that would be impossible to do.

If I chose to go through the treatment, I would need a village to take care of me, relying on friends for traveling to and from treatments, doctor appointments, runs to drug stores for prescriptions, emergency visits to the hospital. And, more importantly, I would need their emotional support so vital to my survival. The thought of dying was nauseating but honestly, it felt a whole lot easier than enduring the treatment I just learned about.

Six

P.I.N.

"War against war is war." We are led to believe that if we apply pressure to unwanted things they will go away. Many believe that pushing against these things will cause them to go away and leave your experience. This is not how the laws of the universe work. And it is obviously not the proof of our experience either, because wars seem to be increasing."

-Abraham-Hicks

It was a huge relief to have had my questions answered. At least I knew the facts and should I choose to live, I now knew what would be required of me. But I had another set of questions that no doctor had the answers to.

I spent the next few days in solitude searching my soul for the answers I needed about which direction to take.

Maybe the cancer has some answers. Maybe I needed to ask *it* the questions. *What is this cancer really about? Why now? Why in my throat and neck?*

In 1985 I had been trained in Transcendental Meditation. Since that time I had been faithful to my practice. I appreciated the benefits of quietude, especially when things seemed to be spinning out of control. The faster the energies seemed to be moving, the more I needed to slow down. In the solitude where God could whisper to me in an otherwise very loud world, there was always a resource of guidance.

Although I knew I needed to travel this path of suffering solo, I was not alone

A friend had shared an internet site called CarePages. It was an interactive blog site where I could update my status as often as I liked. Anyone who wished to follow my journey registered. Registrants also had the option to leave me messages of hope and inspiration. Many people wanted to keep up with my progress, and attempting to keep so many loved ones in the loop was a daunting task for my family. The site became my electronic public diary.

My first CarePage message:

I need your support. I need you to hold the high watch for me and with me. The way I see it…I don't have cancer, I have an opportunity to take a closer walk with God and learn what lessons are here for me. Nothing will be learned by battling. I can only learn the lessons through compassion and a willingness to listen to my higher self.

Please do not feel sorry for me or see me as a victim of cancer. Walk with me on this journey as I am certain there are lessons to be learned for all of us.

Love,
Denise

I knew there was a bigger reason why this was happening. I just couldn't identify it at the time. I didn't know, but I knew God did. Making a deal with God, I dropped to my knees.

Time to pray:

"God…Here's the deal…I surrender, I'll endure the treatment the medical experts are describing as the worst treatment there is for any type of cancer. I place the outcome in your hands. If I am to die then I die, but if I live, it better be good. You and I will co-create a life that allows me to use my life in a big way: to be an inspiration to many."

Befriending my cancer as opposed to battling it was critical to my overall health. Clearly, here was an opportunity for a paradigm shift from the way our culture perceives the healing process.

Entering this new phase of my life, I was so appreciative for the spiritual foundation I had built. My understanding of universal truth that everything in life is by divine design offered me insight that my situation was part of that truth.

My faith was strong and it was being tested.

There is no mistaking how well versed our culture is in "battling" cancer. I couldn't pick up one piece of literature, or search any place on the internet, or speak with anyone regarding cancer without reading or hearing about the "battle." "So and so lost their battle." "This one was battling cancer." Yadda, yadda, yadda.

Obviously, my choice flies in the face of society's approach to cancer.

Until my experience with cancer I had never given much thought to the word, disease. When we "dis" something we distort *and* disrespect it. Dis-allowing ourselves the truth of who we are is a difficult and rigid way to live.

The world is constantly waging war on so many fronts. We wage war on drugs, on poverty, on AIDS, on terrorism, on Iraq, on cancer, and so many other areas.

In my heart of hearts I knew that waging a war with something that was already raging within me would be ludicrous.

"I'm realizing this cancer may be the most profound blessing of my life," I told my friend Andi from Colorado, when she called a few days later. She was a therapist by profession. Sharing the same birthday, we understood each other as only two meticulous, fastidious Virgos could.

During our conversation, I had already shared with her my insights about not wanting to "battle" my cancer. Doing battle with something that was already infuriated and inflamed did not make sense to me. Now I told her, "I want to learn all I can from this experience without fighting with it."

Andi told me about a practice that she used. She suggested I begin a dialogue with my cancer and talk to it as I would to a friend. "Ask the cancer questions," she said, "and write down the answers. Every word."

Andi's suggestion resonated with me because it promised the kind of answers I had been groping for. After we hung up I went out on my deck with pen and pad in hand. I sat in my Adirondack chair, closed my eyes, and slid into a deep meditation. Twenty minutes later, I reached for my pen and pad. I conversed with my cancer like I would a friend, a trusted friend. I was totally honest.

Since we were going to be engaged in intimate dialogue, I thought the cancer and I ought to be on a first-name basis. I named it what it was, a pain in the neck. PIN…it's perfect! I gave PIN a pen, and permission to tell me the truth.

With an open heart and an open mind I began our conversation.

"What are you doing in my body?"

PIN answered: "Hang'n out for a bit."

Hanging out? Like he's killing time before heading out to dinner and a movie? "Why?"

"Just feels like I need to be here."

This answer pissed me off. "I don't need you here."

PIN said: "Oh yes you do. You need me here to slow you down, to bring you to your knees, to help you listen to what it is they want you to know."

They? Who the hell are they? With my voice two octaves higher I yelled, "Why do I need to suffer to hear what they have to say? Why? Why do I need to be reduced to nothingness? No food, no water, no voice, no energy….to learn the lessons *they* want to teach?"

PIN enlightened me: "You have been suffering for a long time. It's your natural state, it's what you know."

As difficult as it was to hear this, there it was…out in the open…. someone else, other than me, knew my secret suffering.

Through tears I whispered: "I don't want to suffer any longer. I don't want to have to go through all this fear, and pain and discomfort."

In a very solemn voice PIN asked: "Are you sure?"

"Sure? No…not really!" As much as I didn't want to suffer I was honestly not sure. At some level I was prepared to suffer. I was prepared for the pain. In a crazy sort of way I looked forward to the deep rest from my life's frenetic routine that would come with the suffering.

PIN hesitated and asked: "Well then how do you expect me to release myself when you won't release yourself from the bondages you so clearly want to keep yourself in?"

"I don't really know how to release myself." What would releasing myself look like? Even though I had done so much work, in so many ways, with so many different forms of therapy, I was unsure how to release myself from whatever it was that had gripped me so tightly.

"Yes you do. You know if you want to release yourself from the suffering or not. You have some victim stuff deep inside that hasn't surfaced and you need to get clear or I'll keep hanging out to help you get clear."

Suddenly exhausted, I said: "Why don't you just get out of my body and leave my process to me?"

PIN said: "I *am* your process!!! You need to get it, truly get it. We can do some good work that needs to be done. Stop thinking about what is good for all – it's for the good of you. Once your good gets handled, the good of all will get handled. STOP focusing outward and bring it home to yourself."

Enraged I shouted: "I am pissed this is happening in my life now. In a way I can't believe it! What do you want me to do about you?"

"I want you to do nothing about me. I want you to do nothing about me. I want you to do nothing about me. Go about being for you. Be all you can be. Stop waiting, stop wasting time and stop beating yourself up for nothing."

I was taken by surprise when PIN demanded this of me. "I'm *not* beating myself up for nothing!"

"Really?" PIN snorted, "It doesn't feel that way in here."

Oh my God, of course it didn't. I had been beating myself up. And I was unaware of just how often and how much damage it was doing.

I asked: "What do you need for you to be on your way, truly gone from my temple?"

PIN imparted true wisdom: "Start treating your temple like the sacred place it is. Honor all levels, all aspects and honor all you know. Stop with any nonsense and love yourself unconditionally.

The more you love yourself the less reason there is for me to be here. The more light you can hold, the less room there will be for me."

Whoa! Those last two lines held my life in them.

PIN's messages were hard to digest. Embodied in them was the freedom I was desperate for. Something major had happened. I felt it. The unmistakable and undeniable need for self love was at the heart of Ambassador PIN'S message.

This dialogue had altered my life. The more I surrendered, the more the communication flowed. It truly felt like I had been in a conversation with another human being. The guidance transcended my own thought process. I knew it from deep within, where all-knowing dwelled. This guidance proved critical to my healing.

I realized PIN was conceivably more evolved than I, and I was humbled. I dove deep into self-discovery.

Curing was the work of the doctors, but healing me from the inside out would be the work of my soul.

Seven

Take a Good Look in the Mirror

"God sleeps in the rocks,
Awakens in the plants,
Walks in the animals,
and knows itself in humans."

- Old Indian Axiom

For the love of God, could it really be that simple? Was self love the key element to healing? I had been struggling and I didn't realize just how much. Apparently, I had been competing in a playground of mental gymnastics. The nagging thoughts of self doubt, self criticism, judgment and second guessing myself had been termites that had eaten away at me.

The heart-to-heart with PIN had hit the emotional lottery for me. Now, the million dollar question, *What was in the way? What was in the way to loving myself unconditionally? Where should I begin? How could someone who has done as much emotional and spiritual work as I burrow into my soul in a new way and peel away yet another layer?* I felt I had opened a doorway to my soul, I had never known existed.

Fortunately, it was time for Marc's shaman class. Shaman class was a safe place for self exploration and a place to explore these questions. During the last class Marc felt my illness was possibly the portal I needed to access my life purpose and that I was on the threshold of something big.

Shaman class had always included meditation and self-reflection. Marc had known my ability to lead the class in sound healing exercises always brought the group into meditation at a deep level.

On this particular day, Marc asked if I would lead the class using a sound healing technique. I referred to the technique I had learned from Jonathan Goldman of using sound to balance and align our chakras.

A chakra is a center of activity that receives, assimilates, and expresses life force energy. The seven main chakras are housed within our torso up to our head along the spinal column. Our base chakra, the first of the seven, is between our legs. The second chakra is just below our navel, third is at our solar plexus, fourth is at the center of our chest, fifth is at the base of our throat, sixth is in the center of our forehead, and the seventh is at the crown of our head.

The sound of "AH" opens the heart chakra. Spiritual love, compassion and kindness are all connected to the heart chakra. Many prayers and sacred names hold the sound of "AH" within them for example; Amen, Allah, Alleluia, Yahweh, and many others. Suffice it to say the sound of "AH" is a sacred and powerful sound.

As the group's voices wove the sound of "AH" I felt the energy build to an intense level. Our voices wove the fabric of our universal oneness.

Then we entered the silence. Within moments a vision of the Blessed Mother appeared before me. Beside her were long flowing white sheets, supple, sheer sheets of linen. I could smell the scent of clean fresh air that lingered in the linen. Hundreds and hundreds of these sheets layered, hanging like sheets drying on a clothes line on a breezy summer's day.

The Blessed Mother reached out her hand; she pulled aside the linen that created a portal into a panoramic scene: lush greens, rolling hills, blue sky, an expansive variety of trees, the colors could not be described.

The Blessed Mother looked at me. I heard these words, "If you all had any idea how much God loves you, and how much love there is for you, you would never worry about another thing again."

As I returned from meditation, I felt I had been released from any worry, possibly for the rest of my life.

I felt the enormity of the moment. This message was for each person in the room. I was the messenger that had to share it with my classmates. Each one was brought to tears by my sharing. This was something to internalize and apply to our lives. This was a true gift from Spirit. Personally, this was a marker, a place where I began paying closer attention to my thoughts around worry.

By kismet, one of my favorite quotes had always been from the Gospel of Luke 12:22

DO NOT WORRY

"Then Jesus said to his disciples: "Therefore I tell you, do not worry about your life, what you will eat, or about your body, what you will wear. Life is more than food, and the body more than clothes. Consider the ravens: They do not sow or reap, they have no storeroom or barn, yet God feeds them. And how much more valuable you are than birds! Who of you by worrying can add a single hour to his/her life? Since you cannot do this very little thing, why do you worry about the rest?"

***

Several friends had offered suggestions about healing modalities they firmly believed in. My good friend, Barbara, had worked with a healing master named Chun. Barbara offered to pay for a session to determine if this modality would resonate with me, and if Chun was someone who could assist me on *my* journey.

Feeling protective of myself I was hesitant to say yes to anything immediately. Because I was so familiar with many different modalities, it was important to me that the person be clear, confident and gifted in their field. I contemplated this particular kind of healing and read some about it on the internet and it felt right. I accepted Barbara's invitation.

Barbara was not only generous in her gift but she also transported me to the appointments.

The healing sessions took place on the floor, which was imported from Korea. The materials in the floor's composition had been proven to promote healing. The color of the floor was a welcoming tawny color, and it was very spongy and comfortable to lie on.

Chun was a tiny woman who could not have weighed more than ninety pounds. Her brown eyes were clear and her hair was short and flat to her head.

She sat next to me on the floor yogi style and placed her hands on my abdomen.

Then she began tapping the center of my chest with the tips of her right hand. Ever so gently, ever so quietly, with the sweetest accent, she repeated the words, "Be in bo-dy, be in bo-dy, be in bo-dy."

My mind was extremely active. By calling my attention to my heart with her tapping, she invited me to travel a more tranquil and peaceful path from head to heart.

The principles of this type of healing are simple; energy follows your mind, moves your blood and makes creation in reality. Through stabilizing your physical health, you will purify emotional energy, leaving a clear mind that will light up spiritual energy and bring your mind to the present moment. The complexity lies in the personal application of the principles to ones life.

Chun's repetitive tapping escorted me directly into the present moment.

Following the treatment I felt a deep sense of peace. More balanced and energized.

Barbara offered to pay for another session, and so Chun and I met the following week.

The second session followed a similar format. She began tapping and asked questions about my life.

"What your nationality? How old are you? You have grandparents alive? Your parents alive? What your relationship like with family? With father? What was father like? How old when he died? How old mother when she died?"

Then she asked an interesting question, "Your father do best he can do?"

My response was immediate and less than loving, "NO...he did not."

My father was old school Italian. I loved my Dad, but we didn't always see eye to eye. According to my father, children should be seen but not heard and women belonged in the kitchen, barefoot and pregnant. He saw no reason for me to attend college because it would only be a waste of money. Marriage and raising a family were the appropriate choices for a woman. My translation? My parents didn't have the money to send me to college and didn't have the insight to support my ambitions so they strongly dissuaded me.

This session opened a scar that I thought had been healed, but it required additional attention.

Once my ranting about my father not doing his best ceased, in her soft Korean accent she affectionately asked,

"Do you think you do best you can do?"

"Yes, I do think I am doing the best I can do." She then posed the question,

"Then why you not think father do best he can do?"

The moment those words passed her lips, energy rushed through me like the force of a river after a long winter thaw. In that moment I realized we are all doing the best we can do, and my *father* was no exception.

Forgiveness became my priority. It was where I began the process of unconditional self-love as PIN had suggested. I had to begin with forgiving myself.

Forgiveness was a gift only I could open. Over time I learned forgiveness was not about the other person, it was about me. It was an opportunity to "give for" to give for another way of looking at things. To forgive was a liberating experience for my own spirit. It cultivated a tranquil inner landscape. The ill feelings inside me for another person caused damage to me, not them. The feelings I harbored around my father had destroyed *my* sacredness, not his.

Time to pray:

Mother/Father God — Divine Presence, the one powerful omnipotent God-hear me now that I am forgiven. That I may forgive anyone and everyone who ever moved in my life in a way that was not seemingly for my highest and best. Thank you God for helping me forgive myself.

For this I am grateful and I release and let go of all that does not serve me. In this now moment I am free from all past hurts and past wounds.

The power of prayer in my life had been palpable. Forgiving could be simple. The thoughts of not being enough, not having enough, not doing enough, were just old tapes that could be re-recorded.

I remembered reading about a type of healing process in Louise Hay's book, "You Can Heal Your Life" that was worth exploring.

Louise started what would become her life's work in New York City in 1970. She attended meetings at the Church of Religious Science and began training in the ministerial program. She became a popular speaker at the church, and soon found herself counseling clients. This work quickly blossomed into a full-time career. After several years, Louise compiled a reference guide detailing the mental causes of physical ailments, and developed positive thought patterns for reversing illness and creating health. This compilation was the basis for *"Heal Your Body"* also known affectionately as "the little blue book." She began traveling throughout the United States, lecturing and facilitating workshops on loving ourselves and healing our lives.

Louise was able to put her philosophies into practice when she was diagnosed with cancer. She considered the alternatives to surgery and drugs, and instead developed an intensive program of affirmations, visualization, nutritional cleansing, and psychotherapy. Within six months, she was completely healed of cancer.

If it worked for her why couldn't it work for me?

In 1980, she began putting her workshop methods on paper. In 1984, her new book, *"You Can Heal Your Life"*, was published. In it, Louise explained how our beliefs and ideas about ourselves are often the cause of our emotional problems and physical maladies and how, by using certain tools, we can change our thinking and our lives for the better.

One of the practices she offered was to say, "I love you," while looking into a mirror.

As I approached the mirror in my bathroom my heart pounded. I felt as if I was meeting a potential lover for the first time. I looked into my eyes and it was not easy. I felt shaky and looked away. I felt internal movement I had never felt, as if someone attached electrodes to the tip of each of my cells. My arms were tingling and my legs felt wobbly. Again I looked away.

And again I approached the mirror and gazed a bit longer. I was able to look into my eyes for 15 seconds before I needed to look away. This wasn't an easy exercise.

How often had I looked in the mirror but never really looked at *me*? It had always been my face, my teeth, my hair, my makeup, but I never looked deep into my own eyes.

I wanted desperately to be able to look into my eyes and tell myself I loved myself but I stood there with my head bowed, as if ashamed. Two minutes passed, three minutes passed. Again I looked up, but this time when I looked into my own eyes there were tears filling my eyes. They streamed down my cheeks. I placed my hands upon the mirror and embraced my reflection. My eyes penetrated to my soul and I said,

"I love you…I love you…I love you, Denise." I fell to the floor. I curled up into a ball and cried a tarn of tears.

Although it had exhausted me, I knew this was an exercise that deserved my attention. It was fundamental to my healing. As time passed, looking deep into my soul became less arduous. I was a beloved child of God and therefore deserved to feel the love that God had for me.

I was ready, truly ready, to release whatever blocked my feeling forgiven and loved. I was ready to release whatever prevented me from forgiving myself, for whatever it was that I had conjured in my head and harbored in my heart about not deserving God's love and the deep love that I deserved to have for myself.

I got much better at mirror work. There was more room inside me. I felt lighter and less congested. My connection to the Divine had intensified. I felt as if God was breathing my breath with me. I felt happier than I had ever felt. And I had been an intrinsically rather happy woman.

During one of the "love" sessions, I had decided to apply a bit of lipstick and not only look at myself in the mirror and say I love you, but, kiss myself as well.

I placed my lips against the mirror, looked into my big brown eyes, kissed myself, held the kiss, and peered deeply. I saw the child. I saw the wounded one, I saw the one who deserved my loving care.

I decided to leave my lips imprinted on the mirror. Reminding me every time I entered that room I also entered my inner sanctuary and loved myself a little bit more.

I embraced the child within. This exercise became easier with each passing day as it became part of my routine. And my mirrors......well.... they were a mess, but I liked them just that way.

- Eight -

I Want to Know my Mask

"I want God to play in my bloodstream, the
way sunlight amuses itself on water"

Elizabeth Gilbert

It was time for another full moon fire ceremony so I headed to Marc's house. It came at the perfect time for me, and was yet another sign from the universe that all was in Divine order.

In just a few days I would be undergo surgery at Salem Hospital so that doctors could insert the feeding tube.

I looked forward to offering fear, worry, concern, and anger to the fire, and receiving its cleansing heat that evening.

Most attendees at the ceremony were aware of my recent diagnosis. I could feel their pain and their fear. They grieved and already missed me even though I was standing in front of them. I sensed the intensity of their feelings the moment I set foot on that sacred ground. The evening was crisp and clear. And the smell of the smoke brought me home to mother earth.

At the southern entrance I dropped to my knees and was enveloped in the energy of the flames. Calling forth all spirit guides, saints, ancestors, angels, animal spirits, and Goddesses, I bowed to the fire in gratitude knowing my spirit helpers were all there to bolster the energy of healing. The song of my heart found its way out my mouth, and the participants began to drum and chant their own song in support of my time at the fire.

Marc knelt down beside me and whispered, "It's all Spirit. You are Spirit. You don't need to do anything to be worthy of healing."

I was a child of God and for that reason alone I was worthy. Quieting those voices did not have to be arduous. I didn't have the energy for arduous any longer. Softening in all areas of my emotional life was what would heal me. This truth struck a chord in me and I began to cry.

As I sobbed my friends began to sob too. Their heartache was written all over their faces. Moments like these remind us of our own mortality. The possibility of losing someone special cleanses the lens we often look through. It encourages us to focus on what is important and what to prioritize.

Time to pray:

Great Spirit, you support in being enough. I trust the process and cast any unworthiness into the hands of God. I release and let go. Trusting my internal wisdom and strength I move forward knowing I am worthy of being healed.

I am worthy because you love me. Staying present to this truth keeps me closer to you. Being closer to you dissolves anything that stands in my way of healing.

The next day I headed to Salem Hospital. I was feeling remnants of the fire ceremony. Any doubts I had about the impending surgery were resolved. I trusted it was part of the healing process.

Though not a fan of this hospital, experience had taught me that insurance ruled, and often times governed, treatment destinations. I needed to be here because it was connected to the center where I would eventually receive chemo and radiation.

The insertion of the feeding tube would take only an hour, so general anesthesia was not necessary. Versed, the drug used to sedate me, would give me the sensation of being under general anesthesia but carried far less risk. As long as I was unaware of the doctor drilling a hole through my abdomen into my stomach, I was good with it.

Marsha and I had already strategized to make our escape by dinner time…at the latest.

I'm not quite sure the doctor performing the procedure was old enough. Somehow these docs resembled kids, which was a bit unsettling. The "upside" of that was, he was newly minted from medical school. I would hopefully reap the benefit of the latest and greatest medical discoveries and techniques.

The operating room was bright with cheery yellow walls. A nurse approached me with a small red plastic box. I was becoming familiar with this box that contained all the supplies needed to extract blood and to infuse me with any required fluids. She snapped a stretchy rubber band on my arm. Within minutes I was traveling inter-dimensionally.

What seemed like only seconds later, I opened my eyes to see the reassuring face of my best friend in the entire world...Marsha. I always felt safe knowing she was in the fox hole with me.

After a few hours the sedation began to wear off and I began to writhe in pain. The nurses were flabbergasted. That simple procedure generally induces just minimum pain in 99% of patients.

Well I guess I was in the darn one percent!

These docs had no idea what had caused my fiery red hot pain at the incision right above my navel. They could only deduce that they may have unintentionally nicked my intestines while making the incision.

One of the doctors informed me that most often they were performing that operation on elderly people who were out of shape. In my case, all the sit ups and strength training I had done was contributing to the pain because they cut through muscle that was taut and isn't responding well to the incision. Go figure!

Nothing helped the pain to subside. The doctors decided to keep me overnight for observation to determine the cause of my discomfort. Because of the lengthy wait for a room assignment Marsha and I remained in the recovery room. I glanced over at Marsha whose face had a look of despair. We were supposed to be at just the beginning of a complex treatment protocol. This was supposed to be the easy part and here I lay with pain contorting every part of my body.

My tolerance for pain had been herculean. Often I had been able to "breathe through" physical pain, but no amount of breath work, transcendental meditation, or application of spiritual knowledge was softening the pain I felt now.

Finally escorted to my room, I met the nurse who would be caring for me that evening. She seemed younger than the attending physician. I swear this girl graduated nursing school a few minutes ago.

Neither she nor Marsha had any idea how to help me ease my pain, so I suggested someone fetch me a face cloth. When Marsha questioned my request, I said, between clenched teeth, "I want to tie it in a knot so I can stick it in my mouth, and when the pain gets unbearable, I am going to bite down on it."

Unfortunately, Marsha was unable to stay with me throughout the night. I wasn't happy she had to leave me in this condition, but I guessed I had better suck it up and get used to it because I had a long road to travel and there wasn't always going to be someone beside me to share the load.

Praying had always comforted me. At that point, I was in such pain I could not focus even for a moment to pray.

This was going to be a long night. And Nurse Nancy had a look on her face that said, "I'm not sure I chose the right career."

Finally, because I was so physically tortured by the pain the nurse gave me drugs to at least help me relax.

Just about the time I began to settle down, two nurses wheeled me to the CAT scan machine for imaging. This test would rule out the possibility of any internal bleeding. The CAT scan took an hour and I was returned to my room. I was so tired I just wanted to sleep. I began to fade off so I closed my eyes and whispered a few prayers.

The light of day was peeping through the blinds when I awoke a few hours later. The pain, while not gone, had subsided a little to where I no longer needed to bite down on the face cloth but I was still physically and emotionally exhausted from my ordeal.

I heard what sounded like familiar footsteps in the hall. I started to cry just thinking, *Could it possibly be my sister?* In a moment she came through the door. I wasn't alone; my big sister had come to comfort me.

Deleta hit her right thigh once with her fist, the way she does when she is more than angry. "Oh my God honey, look at you. What the heck happened? The doctors said this was going to be the easy part?"

"I know. I was sure we would be in and out of here in no time yesterday. Instead, I'm still here in so much pain, I can barely stand up. Promise me you will never leave me alone overnight again?"

Deleta kissed me on the forehead, "I promise."

***

With only one day's rest, my first radiation treatment was scheduled at North Shore Cancer Center (NSCC). I was still in pain from the surgery, and was nervous about having to lie flat on my back during the treatment.

Unfortunately, Marsha was not able to join Deleta and me on my first day of radiation.

But, a few weeks prior, Marsha drove me to North Shore Cancer Center (NSCC) so I could be fitted for my mask. The nurse at the center told me to be prepared to be in the mask for over an hour and a half while they set up how they would target the radiation. I was terrified.

Marsha and I were brought into a CAT scan room. Through the glass window on the opposite side of the room stood a huge, eight foot dashboard displaying a myriad of colorful blinking lights.

Dr. McIntyre was my radiation oncologist, whom Deleta described as "eye candy." He was sitting at the dashboard looking serious while studying my chart.

The technician said, "Please lie on the gurney and please don't move. We need to take this large piece of plastic and place it over your face. At first it will feel warm and it will be very wet, but don't panic, it will quickly cool down. It has a lot of fluid on it so you cannot breathe, open your eyes, or your mouth until I say so"

I nodded, "Okay."

The technician allowed Marsha to assist her. They placed the sopping wet blanket of plastic on my face and the technician began to mold it to my face, tucking it under my neck, shaping it over my nose, my mouth, my ears, my eyes, and my chest. She pulled the plastic away from my mouth and announced, "Okay, breathe through your mouth only."

Whew, I was seconds away from a panic attack.

This procedure was the first critical step in the radiation process. Once the mask was sculpted to my face, I need to remain masked, snapped onto the gurney, and backed into the CAT scan machine for one and a half hours while Dr. Mac mapped the radiation beams.

Now that I was here for the first actual day of radiation, I realized the technician and Marsha had done a fantastic job. The mask was a perfect fit. In fact, the mask was so snug, within moments after they fastened it down to the gurney with me in it all my claustrophobic issues swamped me.

This was a learning moment for me. I learned the importance of trusting my own inner knowing and how important it was to act upon it. I had often dismissed my truth because I didn't want to cause upset. Now more than ever I needed to honor my truth. I knew the only way to survive these treatments was to form a personal relationship with my mask.

"Please take this off me right now, I said. I need a little time with that mask. I have no relationship with it. If it is all the same to you, and I don't disrupt your schedule, I would like to take this mask out into the lobby and get to know it."

The technician had a puzzled look as if she had never heard anybody say anything like that before. When my sister Deleta saw me coming through the door with the mask in hand, she had the same perplexed look on her face. I explained,

"I need to feel what it feels like to have it on without being anchored to a gurney."

I proceeded to stand against the wall putting pressure against the edges of the mask so I could feel the feeling of being restrained but knowing I could release myself. I began a conversation in the waiting room with an elderly man who was watching Oprah. With my new best friend "the mask" while I held the mask against my face, he and I chatted about what was on today's show. He thought my, "getting to know my mask," idea was brilliant and very humorous. It seemed to help alleviate some of his nervousness about his impending treatment.

Thirty minutes later, after getting used to feeling what it felt like to have this contraption against my face, I felt more relaxed than I did at first pass. My mask and I returned to the control room.

They had never had a patient make that type of request. My need to familiarize myself with the mask gave the technicians an idea worth sharing with future patients.

As I reentered the radiation room, I heard the familiar sounds of my Native American flute music. Earlier, I had given the technicians a cassette tape of some favorite music to create a familiar, calming atmosphere during my treatments. I was ready!

Once again the techs fastened me down, and everyone exited the room. I was totally alone with a monster of a machine that would zap the hell out of me. I decided to keep my eyes shut. I sensed the gigantic piece of machinery. It whined at me. It sounded similar to the Indy 500 when the announcer bellows, "Ladies and gentlemen, start your engines."

Suddenly, I felt its breath closing in on the left side of my neck. A few minutes later the breathing moved to the front of my face and remained for what seemed eternity, then cranked itself over to the right side of my neck and eventually back behind my head, to home base.

Moments later my entourage of helpers and loved ones appeared with encouraging cheers of "Good for you…you did it."

I did it, and I'd be back tomorrow to do it all over again.

This was only the first day of forty days to endure this torture.

Although I loathed the mask, I had a suspicion I may grow to love the radiation techs. Their warmth, understanding and loving-kindness was extraordinary, and I appreciated them.

When I returned home I felt agitated. Something uncomfortable stirred inside and had reared its ugly head. I wasn't sure how to deal with the discomfort.

A few weeks earlier, I bought a wiffle ball bat.

Remembering my days of therapy where bats, pads, and pounding devices were used to release anger and stuck emotion, I thought I was going to need one.

Now was the time for my first session.

I suspected underneath whatever these feelings were was a pool of tears, Crazy thoughts and questions raced through my head at breakneck speed

Why do I have to do this? I hate that mask. I can't stand the thought of having to do this tomorrow and the next day and the next day. Maybe I ought to just die? What was this all about? I know I didn't do anything wrong, but it sure feels like I have. I don't deserve this. No one deserves this. I wanted to smash the crap out of anything and everything in my sight. I ought to just get in my car, drive away and never turn back.

Instead of running away I ran to my bedroom with wiffle ball bat in hand. I whacked and whacked and whacked at my pillows and my mattress, screaming out at the top of my lungs all my crazy thoughts.

The incision for my feeding tube began to hurt like hell but I didn't care. The pain of it fueled me. I whacked and screamed, and whacked...whacked... whacked..., pounding my bed with everything I had, until I fell to the floor. I crawled across the floor to the corner of my bedroom and curled into the fetal position. I cried and cried and cried. Tears from years of stuffed feelings from times I had not permitted myself to speak my truth. What I felt or what I needed. Tears from dark places of secrets I never dared to share.

I felt as if every cell of my body was being purged. I took advantage of every opportunity to express whatever it was I felt, especially anger and rage.

It was evident that underneath the anger was an enormous reservoir of sadness and tears. I mustn't take the high road all the time. My spirituality had to make room for my personality by allowing me to express my emotions that weren't always loving. I could not let my understanding of universal law get in my way. I didn't need something kicking me to a higher ground so I would "get all spiritual." I needed to be right there in the thick of everything I was feeling.

All was in divine order. That was true. But that day I didn't give a damn about all that. Right then I needed to honor my truth. On some obscure level I had a restless feeling that I subconsciously promoted this condition – not sure why. Sometimes I had felt bored here on earth. I loved people, but what else did I love? Why had I been bored? I remember asking a rhetorical question to the universe, "How many more times do I have to eat breakfast?" Not sure why this was a question but it had occurred to me the universe had been listening and my higher self had found a way to eliminate my concern.

The next day was my first day of chemo. I had always sworn I would never allow the slow drip of chemotherapy to flow through my veins. In fact, chemo always fell into the same category as the MRI machine. Never!

I took my Aunt Florrie's advice. She had been diagnosed with lymphoma and was cured by chemo. She suggested I imagine that the chemo was holy water flowing through me, blessing me, anointing and healing me from the inside out.

Marsha and I arrived at the center early and ready to meet the chemo team. A young man approached and escorted us into a large, long room with several bays separated only by curtains. Each bay had been equipped with an oversized leather recliner, a silver pole with several bags of fluid hanging, a folding chair, and a small television with the remote control set on the recliner.

I was directed to sit in the recliner. I had been told the major side effect of chemo was nausea. I hadn't even had any and I was already ready to vomit. I looked at Marsha and remarked, "Are we sure I want to do this?"

Marsha assured me we needed to do it, and it would be over soon.

The familiar red plastic box arrived for the ceremonial implanting of the IV needle.

After inserting the intravenous needle into my arm, the technician said, "Before we can start the chemo drip I need to give you some Benadryl. In case you have an allergic reaction to the chemo, we will be ahead of it."

He was the expert, so I just nodded. What he didn't tell me was *how much* Benadryl he was administering. After a few minutes he switched the hookup and started the chemo. Marsha's eyes grew wide as she watched me watch that poison flow into my veins. Not thirty minutes into it and my body began to twist, contort, and flail. My legs stiffened and my arms involuntarily flailed about my head.

"Knock it off Mona." Marsha commanded. "Knock it off" was her default order when she didn't like what was happening.

I got scared, I thought I was having a seizure, "I'm not sure why I am doing this Marsha, I have no control. What the heck is happening?" I realized I was in a serious predicament. Marsha summoned the technician politely because she didn't want to cause a scene.

71

With one look at me he blurted, "Oh dear. You are having a reaction to the Benadryl. This happens to maybe one in every one thousand people."

I insisted he get the prescribed antidote and reverse what was happening to me.

Apologetically he said, "I can't. There is nothing I can do. You'll be okay. It just has to wear off. In about an hour or so your body will relax and will most likely be exhausted."

Geez, first complications with the feeding tube and now this? Clearly I was not included in the law of averages.

An hour passed. I was exhausted but the writhing had stopped. I did my best to keep my left arm straight so the chemo could flow easily. I curled up in the recliner and fell asleep.

Five hours later Marsha woke me, "Mona, the treatment is finished honey. Once they remove the tubing and IV, we can leave."

Relieved, I said, "Wow! I can't believe I slept through the entire process."

Because of the steroids they gave me during the chemotherapy treatment, I was so energized when I got home I cleaned my house from top to bottom. I felt so strong. My mood was light and I had become a proponent of chemotherapy. I told everyone who happened to call that I loved chemo. By the time the sun had set I felt light headed and had pains in my stomach. Sipping hot water always soothed any discomfort I may have had, but not today. The fetal position on the couch with a pillow pressed against my abdomen was the only way I found comfort.

I dove deep into my inner knowing and took some time in prayer. I contemplated whether or not to return next week or ever again for another chemotherapy treatment.

I had curled myself onto the couch with the clicker in hand and watched some mindless television show. I eventually fell asleep and remained there until morning.

I shuffled into the bathroom the next morning and felt a weird sensation on the side of my neck. Through foggy eyes, I peered in the mirror. Swollen did not come close to describe what I observed. From my jaw bone, down to my collar bone, the swelling of my neck appeared to be the size of an orange. I was so swollen I could barely move my head in either direction without excruciating pain.

I retreated to my recliner and sat quietly, *Mother of God help me. Somebody help me! What is going on here?*

The nausea had subsided since last night but now I didn't know what could possibly be the cause of this swelling. I thought about the mask. Panic set in.

Marsha was on her way to take me to the mask. How would they strap me into something so tight with my neck so swollen? There was no way it was going to fit. Doctor's orders had been clear that I was not to miss one treatment. Any break in the treatment would have disturbed the magic of the monster machine and its benefits.

I must soldier on, but this totally sucked!

Marsha arrived promptly at eight, looked at me, and while inspecting my appearance said, "What the heck is going on? Your neck looks swollen."

I responded, "Really...Geez Marsha, I hadn't noticed." My motto, "No matter what...keep your sense of humor." Marsha and I chatted and agreed that the mask was not going to fit.

When we arrived at the cancer center I bypassed the radiation room and headed directly for Lisa, Dr. Mac's nurse. Lisa assessed my appearance and remarked, "Oh no...it looks like you have had some kind of reaction to the chemo and it caused the nodes to get inflamed."

She could tell how frightened and concerned I was. Lisa reassured me that they had seen this type of thing before and that the radiation folks would revamp the mask in such a way that it would not put too much pressure on the swollen area.

The technicians in the radiation department were not concerned. They made the necessary adjustments to the mask. They melted the webbing and stretched it so it was just a bit wider on the swollen side of my neck. Although they had stretched it, the mask was still uncomfortable when they snapped me in. Until the swelling went down, which took the better part of a week, I felt even more claustrophobic because it made it harder for me to breathe during the treatment.

I had a decision to make about whether or not to continue with chemo.

The next morning I woke to the sound of rain tapping on my window. It was an invitation. I love the rain. Most often when the rain came, I suited up and took a walk, loving the cool wet feel of the rain against my skin. It seduced me to walk on for miles.

Today, I was too weak to walk. Instead, I put my raincoat on over my nightgown and perched myself on the deck just outside my living room. Soaked through my raincoat to my pajamas and my under garments I began to chant the sound of "Om," the primordial sound of the universe. Om is the most often chanted sound among all the sacred sounds on earth. This sound is considered to be the sound of existence. Om is considered the humming sound of the cosmic energy.

Often, I was soothed by this simple sound. Over the years of studying sound healing I had used many different forms, but sometimes this simple sound helped the most.

On this day I vibrated to the core with this healing sound, I felt cleansed. I was drenched with both sound and rain. Engrossed in prayer I lost track of time. I asked God to give me a sign to help me to decide. Do I continue with chemo or not? In that moment I was moved to write. I removed my sopping wet clothes, left them on the porch and sat naked just inside the door on the floor with my journal on my lap. I felt a tremendous connection of oneness with God and Spirit.

I wrote:

"RAIN"

The rain is steady. The rain is heavy. It calls to me. I go. I sit in complete darkness feeling every drop. Saturated to my core with God's drink. If I stop listening I can hear every raindrop's song. Singing only for me. I smile, I laugh, I chant.

My oneness is more than a feeling. It is a knowing. Angels dance in the rain all around me. Angels dance in the rain. They know I know. They smile, they laugh, they chant.

Here was my answer. I had made a commitment to myself that I would always trust my knowing. And this was the truth of my knowing. In that moment I was certain there would not be another trip to North Shore Cancer Center's chemotherapy department. Radiation was the only treatment I endured. As certain as I knew my own name, I knew no matter how much resistance I met from family and friends, whose fear may have tried to overrule my decision, I never again allowed the ills of chemotherapy to invade my temple. This time I would say never.

- Nine -

Love Spelled Backwards

---

*"We cannot love without evolving and
we cannot evolve without love"*

-Denise DeSimone

For the year prior to my diagnosis, I was involved with a group of twenty two people from different parts of the country. We studied a type of therapy called Process Therapy. We tagged ourselves The Village People. Every six weeks we gathered for four days at our teacher's home in New Haven, CT.

Throughout the year we explored aspects of our personal, spiritual and professional lives. During an exercise, while I sat on the floor in a contemplative, comfortable crossed-legged position, I was drawn to the large gold letters adorning the wall in front of me. Each letter measured approximately twelve inches tall. They spelled the word love. I began to play with the word, noticing the feelings that surfaced when I thought about the many ways in which I experienced love.

I began to play with the letters as if they were in front of me on a wooden rack like a Scrabble holder. Moving the letters around on the Scrabble board in my head, I spelled love backwards. When I did, it dawned on me...spelling the word "love" backwards, and weaving it through itself, spelled evolve.

Ha! We cannot love without evolving and we cannot evolve without love. Weaving in and out of each other's lives strengthens our love, and loving each other supports our evolving. Of course spelling love backwards would spell evolve. I felt I had unearthed one of the many great secrets to life. I shared my discovery with the group, at which time the teacher smiled a big Buddha smile, chuckled and said,

"Denise, I wish you would stop being so shallow."

I could not possibly have evolved through this health challenge without the love of friends and family. We all evolved through sharing our love for one another.

And self love was the seed place in the process of evolving.

A CarePages update:

Greetings,

All is well.

The power of love continues to blow me away. I don't care how tough it gets (and they tell me it will get even tougher) I will continue to stay focused on the many hearts that are here for me on every level. I would like to say thank you to my "Sweet Susans." My nephews Frank and Tom are married to the most generous and loving women I know. They arrived Friday evening with overnight bags, baby soft "party socks", smiles and so much love in their hearts. Spending the night away from home was not an easy venture for them. They have husbands, children, soccer games, swimming, jobs of their own, and not to mention, live over an hour away. We had a good ole time. Thank you both so much for taking time to be with me.

I have one request. I am in need of a car. The lease is up on my car and I do not want to deal with getting a new car at this juncture of the journey. If anyone out there has knowledge of a beat around car for me to buy for short money, please let me know. I won't need a car, and I can't really drive, but at times, I will be home alone and do not want to be without a means of transportation should I need one.

In gratitude,
Denise

(Another update one hour later)

Hello again,

Life just continues to amaze, astonish, and humble me. Not fifteen minutes after I sent out the request for a car my phone rang. It was a friend of mine checking in. One of the things she said (not having seen my last update) was, "Denise, if you need anything at all, let me know." She named several options for helping and one option was the use of her car while she was away in Florida. How perfect life is and how the universe always provides. Susan, thank you for your generosity and friendship. God is good….all the time.

A message from Deleta:

WOW!!! The miracles we can do.

Hi Denise, I can't believe the car story. Oh yes I can…we work wonders with our faith. Melanie showed me this sight so that I can be a part of all this wonder. I can't wait to come and stay with you next week. Together we will make more miracles happen.

I love you,
Deleta

I made updating the CarePages my daily ritual. The sweet love from the honeybees in my life as they sent me personal messages warmed my heart, and offered comfort.

As humans we inherently want to participate. Our individual reasons may differ, but we want to pay it forward and offer support especially when one of the tribe is in need.

These loving and caring messages fueled me to carry on. I had been chosen to be a messenger, and this challenge with cancer was how God chose to catch my attention. These words lifted my spirit like the jet engines that lift a Boeing 747 into the atmosphere.

The supportive messages of love from friends and family buoyed me when I sank into self pity.

Time to pray:

Great Spirit, from this day forward I cherish my body, my life, myself. Through self love nothing will disturb or take that away. I am here to be the way of God, not in the way of God. There is room in my body for only love. Nothing is allowed in my body but love.

It's time. The only thing that's real is love. Faith supports love and allows for a deepening. I dive more deeply into my faith knowing I am held in the arms of Divine love.

It had occurred to me, I had not given much thought to why *I* wanted to stay alive. In the beginning I had given serious consideration to leaving the planet. A part of me felt ready to let my "skin bag" expire. When I decided to live it was based on sparing my family and friends the pain and heartache of losing me. But I had not given too much thought to my own selfish reasons.

Why did I want to stay alive? Sitting quietly with pen and pad, all my reasons effortlessly spilled onto the page. The first reason made an easy smile on my face:

*Because I love the smell of Christmas.

This simple answer rose immediately without edit from a deep and sincere, place within. In that moment I realized how simple life truly was. There was profundity in the simplest expression.

The following list of reasons flowed:

*I love hugging people and looking into their eyes
*I love belly laughing with my dear friend Brooks
*I love to feel rain on my face
*I want to go to Italy time and time again
*I want to become some type of minister
*To continue my daily word and expand it to reach many
*To continue to smile and kiss myself in the mirror
*To get a dog, a really great dog

*To paint from my heart and soul

*I want to write a book

*I want to see the kids growing up

*To be better than I've ever been in every way

*To grow in love day to day

*To master living in the moment.

*To love love, and to let love love me.

I had had an epiphany that I might have complicated too many things in my life. The longer I sat, the more simple life became. Simplicity was the deepest way to live.

Buddhism says it best, "Chop the wood in front of you." No more struggle. Each moment was the only moment. In this now moment all is well. Nothing else mattered.

One of my favorite books is *The Prophet* by Kahlil Gibran. It was published in 1923. The simple complexity of his work would entice me to ponder for long periods of time. The lessons of that book addressed subjects of love, marriage, children, giving, freedom, passion, and several more important topics. One of my favorite chapters defined friendship.

"And youth said, "Speak to us of friendship." And he answered saying: "Your friend is your needs answered. He is your field which you sow with love and reap with thanksgiving. And he is your board and your fireside. For you come to him with your hunger, and you seek him for peace. And let your best be for your friend. If he must know the ebb of your tide, let him know its flood also. For what is your friend that you should seek him with hours to kill? Seek him always with hours to live. For it is his to fill your need, but not your emptiness. And in the sweetness of friendship let there be laughter, and sharing of pleasures. For in the dew of little things the heart finds its morning and is refreshed."

I had come to my friends with my hunger, and they nourished me. And in seeking them for peace, they blanketed me with the warmth of their love. My heart continued to find its morning and was refreshed again and again.

Treatments began to get tougher and I began to experience what those docs had said about how much pain I would have to endure.

***

A CarePages update:

Well, we are halfway there. This coming Wednesday radiation treatments are once to twice a day. This protocol will last for 12 days. That will be the end of radiation. I'm tired. I sleep most of the day away in my new recliner. Thank you again to my sister Diane for such a thoughtful gift.

Dr. Mac says the next phase of radiation will increase my fatigue immensely, and the cumulative effects of burning, sores, and mucus will increase. I have had to surrender even more. These are very hard days for me and I know they are going to get harder.

I appreciate knowing each of you are there helping me through this time

It's astounding what the human body can endure.

Much love,
Denise

Below is a great idea on CarePages from Paula

Dear Denise and all,

An idea came through yesterday when you told us you would have twelve days of radiation twice a day. I would like to propose that we all hold the Twelve Powers in our hearts and minds and souls during that period of time; sending Denise the "swarming" power of our group soul. It can gather the vibration and tone of these powers in an amazing way for all of us.

Below is the schedule and affirmations. They are short and simple so we can easily remember them throughout the day. I suggest using them as a chant that we repeat over and over again.

Wednesday, FAITH (pineal gland) - "Your faith has made you well."

Thursday, STRENGTH (low back) - "I am one with infinite strength."

Friday, LOVE – (heart) "I am one with God, and God was perfect love."

Monday, WISDOM (solar plexus) – "Do not judge by appearances, but judge with right judgment."

Tuesday, POWER (throat) – "All power is given unto me in heaven and in earth."

Wednesday, IMAGINATION (between the eyes) – "My eye is single to the good."

Thursday, UNDERSTANDING (forehead) – "I am the way, and the truth, and the life."

Friday, WILL (upper forehead) – "Not my will, but thine, be done."

Monday, ORDER (navel) – "I am one with the continuous forward movement of the universe."

Tuesday, ZEAL (base of skull) – "I am unified with the energy of the universe."

Wednesday, RENUNCIATION (lower spine) – "My whole being is continually renewed and transformed after the image of the creator."

Thursday, LIFE (generative center) – "I AM RENEWED, RESTORED AND REBORN!"

It is finished.

Let's do this together and allow the powerful energy of prayer to help guide us.

Love to all, Paula

Paula's idea was widely embraced. The tribe was thrilled to have an established, powerful focus.

Charles Fillmore, the co-founder of Unity postulates that as a child of God, we have 12 spiritual powers, each of which manifests and functions in and through a particular part of our body. Fillmore loved to explore science and medicine as ways to explain metaphysical truths and insights.

In Unity we view the twelve powers as spiritual gifts that each one of us can call into expression by the recognition of that particular power. Meditating upon that power and affirming that it is expressing through us supports us in daily life.

- Ten -

In my Quiet World

"It is one of the most beautiful compensations of this life that no man can sincerely try to help another without helping himself."

- Ralph Waldo Emerson

Each passing day brought more clarity. Healing me was directly connected to loving myself and being gentle with myself.

Everything was unfolding according to plan, and not eating sucked in some ways and didn't matter in others. My taste buds were dead from the radiation, so even if I could eat I wouldn't be able to taste anything, so it really didn't matter much.

My kitchen counter, which had once contained a food processor, toaster, and all the utensils necessary to create a gourmet meal, now looked like a laboratory. On many a day, while preparing a meal I would pretend to be on camera taping my upcoming segment on the Food Network. Now, my counter was covered with gauze, syringes, cans of liquid food, pill bottles of every variety and size, and plastic feed bags waiting to be filled and hooked up to my feeding tube.

In my quiet world where I could no longer eat solid food, where I could no longer swallow even water, and often I had no voice, I felt isolated and at times, lonely. Friends and family would feel guilty about eating in front of me. I could understand how they felt, but if they were going to help care for me they needed to care for themselves by staying nourished. It was a difficult time for each of us.

I had a love hate relationship with radiation. All those mysterious zaps were effective and I appreciated that, but the side effects were brutal.

The skin on my face down to my collar bone was burnt. It was as purple as a plum. Deleta and Marsha continuously lathered me with Aquaphor cream to prevent my skin from cracking. Tending to the outside skin was nothing compared to what was going on inside my mouth and throat. Sores, too many to count, had invaded the inside of my cheeks, tongue and gums. Nothing seemed to halt the destruction of my tissue. Speaking was painful. My throat felt as if it was on fire, and I had so many sores on my tongue they had all run together. My tongue hit my teeth when I tried to speak. The pain caused my eyes to sting and tear.

I was thrust against the gutsy commitment I decreed to let my spirit soar no matter how much the treatment destroyed my body. My spirit was soaring though. It seemed the more pain I experienced the deeper the Divine energies invited me to dive into the delicate places of my soul. I could not change anything, so I surrendered again and again. I took one day at a time and did my best to stay in the moment. Often times reducing it to the ridiculous, bowing my head and internalizing this knowing,

I can do this for the next ten minutes. When those ten passed, I said it again, then again, and then again. It was the only way I knew how to deal with the pain.

"So what are you learning from this ordeal?" a friend asked one day.

"People get you through and love is all that matters" I responded.

Although much of what I was learning was still brewing, and many of the lessons were ineffable, my answer to his question flowed easily, like honey in the sun on a warm summer's day.

Several friends and acquaintances offered transportation to and from the myriad of appointments. The healers within my community scheduled times to do reflexology and Reiki. Even my friend Pam came over and painted my toenails, a beautiful ruby red. It took a village!

I allowed people access to my process through the CarePages and it had created a place for their heart-felt contributions which so often was what had kept me going.

A raw CarePage update

Hello to all,

I cannot wait for these radiation treatments to be over and done. Thank God I know God loves me because I have had some cranky moments, meltdown moments and moments of sheer madness over the past few weeks.

My wiffle ball bat (anger management tool) has been in full swing several times. I ended up at the hospital for 10 hours the other day due to an allergic reaction to a morphine patch applied to alleviate the pain. Thank God for Deleta and my friend Katherine, who scooped me off the bathroom floor and whisked me off to the hospital with great intent. It was a "press and pray, everyone please get out of our way" moment.

Good to know I am allergic. I could have met my demise.

Thanks for all the prayers. I need them.

Tons of love,
Denise

An understanding and heart-felt CarePage message from Beth K.

Pain…Now that is a monster that can get in the way of all clear intention and trust, isn't it? Please know that you are allowed to feel furious, impatient, terrified, and even defeated. You know this is not where you live, or where you will stay. But pain, and the kind of pain you must be feeling have a way of bringing its own guest list to the party. So just let them in. They will leave when the snacks are gone and they get bored.

My prayer is this passes quickly and gently, and all the prayers surrounding you through this time act as a soothing bandage. A love patch, whose only side effect is comfort, and the reminder that God is bigger than any and all of this.

We surround you.

Much love,
Beth

Many of my friends had shared with me how my challenge had provided a catalyst for them and encouraged them to reach new levels of self awareness. They became more aware of what they might have taken for granted, the seemingly small things in life. They appreciated each day as the gift it was. What seemed like insurmountable circumstances in their lives had now become portals into self-examination.

This message from Diane G. encapsulated what so many had shared:

Denise, I wanted to thank you from my heart for sharing your day-to-day journey with us all. Your words and hurdles keep me humble, expand my gratefulness, provoke my prayerfulness, and inspire me to return to a perspective that keeps the small stuff out of focus and without power.

You, beautiful child of God, are a glowing torch, a teacher whose path has gathered a circle of students who learn from your every experience. Know that I take these blessed lessons forward into every day with growing wisdom and clarity for having been included.

In love and light I see your body return to its most precious strength and balance.

Love, Diane

This was a time for me to receive and it was also a time for me to give. I kept my heart open and gave my authentic self by being vulnerable.

I was vulnerable to the absence of food. This had encouraged me to explore the different ways I had used food.

Food is celebratory, consoling, a drug of choice, especially candy/sweets. It's a best friend, life sustaining, comforting, and cleansing.

It was all of these and more. I had used food as a mask for my emotions. There were times in my life when it had been easier to avoid my feelings by stuffing them down with food. Now, at a time when emotions were heightened, that was not an option. There was no stuffing or hiding. I was exposed and vulnerable to every emotion.

And, I swear God had granted me some kind of special power for dealing with it because I was not all that crazed. Being with people fed my soul and nourished me in the perfect way during that time.

Deleta asked Dr. Mac if I would be able to eat anything for the upcoming Thanksgiving Day holiday. His response was, "Not this year, but hopefully for many more years to come."

For that Thanksgiving I offered up my forced fasting for children who go hungry day after day after day. Although I did not eat, that may actually have been the best meal I never had. I admitted I missed my niece Beth's pies. She learned from the best, her Nana, my mother.

Upon hearing my lament Beth called to assure me, "Auntie, as soon as you can eat, I will make you as many pies as you can stuff down. I love you."

My family filled me to overflowing.

***

My last day of radiation had finally arrived. I prayed the radiation worked. Soon I would begin strengthening my body and immune system. I felt polluted by so many drugs and wanted to cleanse myself from all the toxins I had absorbed at a cellular level.

Within the next few weeks I would begin alternative treatments that would include the hyperbaric chamber, infrared sauna, colonics and several other treatment options.

Six weeks from now, I would be tested at Mass General Hospital to determine if the cancer had been eradicated. Until then, I visited Dr. Mac weekly so he could chart my progress.

In a strange way I felt an emotional safety in going to the cancer center each day.

I had built a relationship with each of the technicians who had cared for me. They were so gentle and loving. It was evident they loved their work. Helping people like me. I felt safe in their care and I would miss them. Even though it scared the heck out of me to get in that mask every day, I was doing something about the cancer. Now it was a waiting game.

Dr. Mac said once the radiation treatments stopped, the effects would continue and would most likely exacerbate for another month to six weeks. It would take that much time to saturate the cells.

Waiting to be tested to see if the cells were clean felt like limbo. The scary voices of doubt snuck up on me, murmuring -- maybe the radiation didn't accomplish its mission? Would I be faced with having the neck dissection?

***

Six weeks had passed and the results from the PET scan were in. If there had been any sign of cancer then the next step would have been a neck dissection. Just the thought of a neck dissection made me queasy. The scan showed a few places on the back of my tongue that were lit up, but Dr. Mac was not concerned that it was cancer. He saw no need for a neck dissection. This was fabulous news. Beyond fabulous news. When Dr. Mac delivered the news, Deleta and I were hugging and jumping up and down and crying, all at the same time.

But what he did want me to do was to begin sessions with Tessa Goldsmith, a speech pathologist at Mass General Hospital. She and I would work on teaching me to swallow again. Imagine, learning to swallow at age 50?

I had also spoken to Dr. Mac about my intention to enter into alternative treatments, and he was very supportive. The downside of these treatments was the lack of financial support from the insurance industry. Each treatment ranged from fifty to two hundred dollars. The suggested protocol was four to five treatments per week. I prayed the money would appear. I needed to get quiet and listen.

A CarePages update:

Greetings,

I feel I need some time in the silence. Beginning this evening I will be turning off my phone, my computer and my stereo.

Maybe in the silence lies the answer to my prayer as to how I can financially support alternative treatments.

Take good care of yourselves,

Love,
Denise

I trusted I would be guided and I was. I had to stay aware that I could choose to keep reaching for the better feeling thought. That time in the silence had proved beneficial. I had received a fun and clear answer to my prayer.

A CarePages update

Hello to all,

The answer to my prayer has been granted.

I had a wonderful time in the silence resting my voice, meditating, writing, and paying attention to the still small voice inside. There is much information in the silence. The answer to my prayer was given.

I am starting a project that will help me raise some funds. Several years ago I recorded a CD in Nashville, Tennessee with my long time friend, Jess. It contains two original songs and the song, Somewhere Over the Rainbow, a favorite of my mother. During my time in the silence the path to raise funds unfolded.

I am duplicating the CD and offering it for $10 a copy. This is an exciting solution to my problem. I hope you will support me in my efforts to receive treatments which I am convinced will make the difference in not just to survive, but will help me to thrive.

Enjoy your day.
Love, Denise

The response to my CD project was overwhelming. That Sunday the bookstore at Unity on The River featured me as "Artist of the week."

The bookstore manager set up a display of my CDs outside the door of the sanctuary. I sold eighty CDs in one day. People actually requested my autograph, and some folks asked for lipstick kisses on the inside cover.

Additionally, many people ordered multiple copies. People do get you through and love really is all that matters.

Interestingly, I wrote the title track, "Walk With Me," long before my diagnosis. This song had now become my theme song.

The chorus:

Walk with me, Talk with me, Hold the hand of God with me,
Feel the power we share when we are one.

I felt I had been guided many years ago to create that CD for that exact moment in time. In just a few weeks I had raised almost three thousand dollars from the sale of my CD. There was no arguing that all was in Divine order, and that our lives have been mapped out for us. So why resist what is?

I prayed that the blessings my friends and family had bestowed upon me return to them one hundred fold.

How blessed was I!

ELEVEN

The Difference Between Surviving and Thriving

"The truth is that happy people generally don't get sick."

- Bernie Siegel

Based on my preference for alternative and naturopathic medicine, I chose to blend traditional and alternative medicine for a power-packed healing protocol. Herein was the difference between surviving and thriving.

Dr. Mac had said that some of the treatments might protect the cancer while the radiation was trying to eliminate it, so I could not begin alternative treatments until radiation ended.

With radiation behind me, I was ready to begin my alternative treatments. Compared to the hectic pace of the hospital, the subtler energy and familiarity of the naturopathic health clinic soothed me.

Since my last visit of a few years ago, there was a new doctor on staff. Pardon the cliché of tall dark and handsome, but, there's no other way to describe this man. His lanky, six-foot four physique and Abraham Lincoln type chiseled features commanded attention when he entered a room. He had black wavy hair, gentle eyes that smiled long before his mouth did, and an easy laugh.

Dr. Savastio, referred to as Dr. "S" around the naturopathic health clinic, and I hit it off immediately. He appreciated my humor. He also appreciated I was not there as a victim seeking someone to perform magic on me. I was there as an equal, responsible, partner in the process of healing.

First on the vast list of treatments was the hyperbaric chamber. It provided a rejuvenating supply of oxygen to my deprived cells.

When I shared my intentions to use the hyperbaric chamber as a form of treatment, with Dr. Mac, he was well aware of the benefits and said, "This is one of the best things you can do for yourself."

It astonished me that the medical profession understood the benefits of having oxygen forced into my cells, yet had never told me. I was fortunate enough to have had this knowledge and I had to take extreme measures to fund such treatments because the insurance companies in this country rule over a large portion of our country, and chemo is big business.

The clinic had a portable chamber which was less intimidating than the huge chambers that are found in wound centers in hospitals. This one resembled an oversized duffel bag with a long, thick zipper for a spine. There was a small plastic porthole about 5 inches above my face. I would look out and dream I was on a cruise ship because I needed a distraction from being trapped inside this bag for an hour.

The first of many sessions was the toughest. As I approached the bag my knees wobbled. My body shook knowing I had to crawl inside, lie face up, strap an oxygen mask on, and the technician would then zip it shut. I knew there was no immediate escape.

A claustrophobic panic attack was not an option. If I panicked it was an additional ten minutes until the device would decompress, and I would just have to wait it out.

With one foot in the bag and one on the platform beside it, I gazed over at Marsha. She read my mind, and said," Mona, it's this for forty five minutes or five hours of chemo, your choice." I crawled inside.

After the session, once unzipped and freed I felt the effects immediately. I had more energy than I did before I crawled in. I could walk with more stability and strength and the sores in my mouth felt less painful. Being in the chamber was tough because of my claustrophobia but it was a treatment that I learned to tolerate because of the many benefits.

My favorite treatment of all was the warmth of the infrared sauna because I was constantly cold from my body trying to adjust to having lost twenty five pounds.

I would sit on the bench inside what looked like an oversized wooden closet with a glass door. The sweat would pour off me, so I needed several bottles of water to keep myself hydrated. There was the option for piped in music, but I often chose silence because it was a perfect space to meditate.

There were a plethora of treatments offered at the clinic, thirty five in total and Dr. S. and I discussed the ones that would be most beneficial to me.

I would spend a few days each week alternating the hyperbaric chamber, the infrared sauna and some of the others. I would rotate the other treatments weekly.

I was fascinated watching the color of the water of the German footbath turn brown as the toxins began to release from my feet. It had a special combination of herbs and mineral salts that would draw toxins out of my body.

Another, called intravenous infusion, required a needle to be implanted in my vein. Quite a different experience from chemo. This IV needle provided a direct means of feeding specific nutrients that included high doses of vitamin C and a blend of nutrients imported from Germany that nourished my cells instead of killing them. After this treatment I could almost hear my cells whispering, "Thank you."

In addition to visiting the center, my friend, Peter generously offered in-home Reiki treatments and my friend Dan came over weekly to do reflexology on my feet.

Within minutes of Dan touching my feet I would be asleep. I was grateful to Dan for helping me relax during this wearisome time in my life.

The in-home treatments were such a gift because for all other treatments I had to arrange transportation. I had to get myself up and ready to go out and oftentimes it was a struggle to muster the energy I needed. I liked being home in my pajamas and in my comfortable recliner, but I knew I would benefit greatly from the treatments that were helping to rebuild my immune system.

In addition to sessions at the center, weekly acupuncture, and Tong Ren sessions with Tom Tam, and the gifts of my private Reiki and Reflexology sessions, I had been working with a flower essence guru, David, learning about the benefits of essences.

The intelligence within the structure of flowers is amazing. Their determination to push forth regardless of obstacles, the inherent beauty they reflect, and their sacred geometric shapes, had always fascinated me.

The founder of flower essence therapy was an English surgeon named Dr. Edward Bach. Bach was a pioneer in understanding the connection of our emotional bodies to our physical health.

The 38 original flower remedies, known as Bach Flower Remedies, were used to treat the underlying emotional causes of diseases. This quote by Bach speaks volumes: "No knowledge, no science is necessary apart from the simple methods described herein; and they who would obtain the greatest benefit from that God-sent gift would be those who keep it pure as it is; free from science, free from theories, for everything in nature is simple."

My first session with David was notable.

David had been a skilled, certified flower essence practitioner with over 20 years of experience. Through a thorough examination and his gifted, keen intuition, David honed in on six essences for that day's treatment. One in particular was blackberry lily. This one he suggested would support me in releasing old patterns and negative recordings I was holding onto around not making the right decisions in my life.

David also suggested there might be unresolved traumas that had occurred throughout my life, dating back to childhood that needed to be excavated, processed, and released.

He had applied a few drops of his magic potion under my tongue, and I felt a tingling sensation throughout my body. The words to a song I learned long ago rushed in. "Every little cell in my body is happy, every little cell in my body is fine. Feel so good, felt so fine, every little cell in my body's Divine."

I felt divine and I also needed to heed his suggestion and allow the essences to support me in uncovering what David mentioned about my childhood.

Being the youngest of five, with the next oldest eight years older than I, meant that a lot of the time, through no fault of their own, the other kids didn't want me around. It seemed to me that I was tolerated because I fetched and carried. I was the one who was told to get up to change the channel.

From an early age I felt I was only worth having around so long as I was doing something for someone else. I felt like I wasn't good enough to be accepted for just being me.

My parents were in their mid-forties when they had me and for many years I heard that I was "a mistake." As a child I didn't understand what it meant but I knew it sounded bad. During my teen years it all made sense when I began to understand sex.

My parent's explanation to me when I confronted them about my being a "mistake" was, "Oh no honey, we intended to have you so there would be someone to take care of us when we got older."

Great!!! I think I would rather have been a mistake.

There were other traumas and abuses from my childhood and young adulthood that bubbled up to the surface for me to heal. The details are unimportant but I speak of it here because children who have been traumatized almost always feel that they did something wrong.

In the therapy I had done previously, I hadn't always approached the process of exploring the past from a loving kind place. Now cancer was softening me around self examination.

The flower essences were an effective approach. Unearthing the old patterns, negative recordings, and deep seeded traumas would need to be a gentle process and would unfold with simple profundity. Each day I moved closer and closer to feeling that I loved my body and I trusted its wisdom.

I was thankful for having been able to reap the benefits of several therapies that most people who are sick may not be aware of or have access to.

My theology regarding healing is that everything is vibration. Healing occurs energetically. If I didn't take the path of healing energetically, I was not certain I would heal physically.

During additional sessions with Chun, my Korean healer, she sowed more seeds for me to water. The water, most often, came in the form of tears.

Chun had suggested there was ice around my heart and in my system. And it was time to let it melt. I needed to get out of my head and really feel my body.

Again she escorted me into my body with her continuous tapping. In her sweet accent when she repeated, "Sun is master...sun is master." I began to feel my body temperature rise. My entire body shook as I felt the ice melt.

As she continued tapping, she offered other suggestions;

"I am enough...No judgment...Flowers bloom every cell of me... others judge, does not matter."

She taught me that memories would always be there, but they could be invited guests instead of being my master. Her teaching was powerful. I realized judgment could be replaced with curiosity. I could be forgiving instead of holding on to an old pattern that didn't serve me.

The more I experienced forgiveness the more I felt the ice melt away. Over time years of protection and disappointment melted away like remnants of frozen winter at a river's edge.

I saw evidence the day I visited my sister Diane that the changes in me that forgiveness had made were real.

There was a photo of my Dad on a small table in her living room. As I passed by the photo, I picked it up and kissed it. For the first time in a long time, I was in touch with how much I missed my father. I felt sad, and at the same time, it felt good to feel my heart missing him.

I was sad that he and my mother were deceased. And the juxtaposition of wanting them alive to hold me through that trying time and being grateful they were deceased was strong. I never would have wanted them to have to witness me suffer, yet at the same time my heart had ached to be held by them.

***

One of the side effects of radiation was a systemic yeast condition called thrush. I was a mess. I had yeast wreaking havoc in my mouth with sores that itched and I constantly cleared my throat.

One day a light bulb went off; if PIN offered such profound guidance, then quite possibly, if I engaged in a similar practice with this annoying yeast, it might shed some light on the situation. I thought of a name to tag the yeast. "Aaa-chem," seemed appropriate.

My first question – "Aaa-chem, what are you doing in my body?"

Aaa-chem's response – "Living"

Demandingly I said – "I need for you to die."

Aaa-chem asks – "Why would I want to die – do you want to die?"

I said – "Absolutely not, and I feel like I might because of you being so present in my body. I feel like you have taken over."

Aaa-chem educates me – "I have not taken over. I could live in your body without being of any discomfort to you."

I asked – "What do I need to do in order to co-exist with you?"

Aaa-chem suggested – "Relax, don't focus on me so much. See me under control. Something is festering that you feel out of control about. It's a good time for you to look at the places in your life where you feel you are out of control."

Uncertain of the process I asked – "Okay, and when I get clearer on these issues, where does that leave you?"

Aaa-chem said – "That leaves me not out of control. I am just an indicator, a way for you to access the deeper parts of your life."

Honestly, I said – "I really need to embrace you and not battle you. This is hard for me. It is so uncomfortable to have you in my mouth and in my throat. At times it is intolerable. It's driving me crazy"

Aaa-chem said – "I know. For that I am sorry. When you take the medicine needed to get me under control, don't think "kill, attack, etc." think "balance, balance, balance." Just like the places in your life where you feel out of control. Discover them and bring them into balance. Balance is the key."

Enlightened by my chat with Aaa-chem and curious about what Louise Hay's list of ailments in her book, "You Can Heal Your Life" had to say. I consulted the book. It listed several diseases and ailments and the correlating issue that might be causing the condition. In addition, she offered affirmations to help one focus on something positive to help usher in a healthier mind/body connection.

Next to the word "thrush" it said "anger over making the wrong decisions." I started to cry thinking about all the seemingly "wrong" decisions I'd made. My tears flowed easily. There was no old reprimanding voice attached to this realization. It just was what it was, a realization and an opportunity to love myself through the process.

The affirmation in the book was "I lovingly accept my decisions, knowing I am free to change. I am safe."

I wove a thread through the work with David and my study of Louise Hay's method and over time I released the demons of the past.

The emotional work I did supported the continued physical work my body demanded.

My time with Tessa, my speech pathologist, was humbling. Here I was 50 years old having to learn how to drink water.

Tessa's South African accent was a pleasant distraction from the arduous work during our sessions. Tessa's straight on stares seemed to peer directly into my soul, and I felt she was searching my soul to see if I had what it took.

Tessa patiently, but firmly, encouraged me to take a sip of water. I would be reduced to tears by fear when I would place a cup to my mouth. A cup to my mouth was foreign. I would break down. I just could not do it. Trying to swallow gagged me. I felt I would choke and drown.

After two sessions it became apparent that therapy was not going to work. My esophagus needed to be surgically stretched. Scar tissue had caused it to close and I simply could not swallow. Unless I had surgery, sustenance would come by way of my feeding tube for the rest of my life.

Fortunately, I was able to get an appointment with the surgeon that same week. My friend Katherine was my transportation and my support person. At the beginning of my whole ordeal we had all decided I was never to go alone to any appointment. It's a good thing I was not alone that day.

While we waited for the doctor to give the one-two rap on the door before he entered, Katherine and I chatted about how relieved we were that there would be no neck dissection.

The doctor's offices appeared to be newly renovated. It seemed they reconfigured the original space in order to transform already tiny treatment rooms into more tiny uncomfortable spaces.

I sat in the center chair, which by its size, position, and headrest was always a give-a-away; it's the patient's chair. Katherine crumpled her tall six foot frame into the small chair to my left just outside my vision. There was just enough room for the doctor to stand a few feet away.

When the doctor arrived he had a stack of papers thick as a phone book clipped together in the upper left-hand corner. While he removed the clip, he launched into an in depth explanation of the extensiveness of a neck dissection. There seemed to be a discrepancy between the results Dr. Mac had given us and what this doctor had deduced from the same PET scan report.

I made a "T" with my hands to signal time out, "Wait. We are here to discuss the procedure to stretch my esophagus. You might have the wrong patient. I don't need a neck dissection."

"From what I see here, these results indicate you do need a neck dissection. If you were under my care, you would be scheduled as soon as possible." He went on to say, "I wouldn't do a stretch on you at this point. Your tissue is much too compromised. I would wait until you were healed. Maybe in another few months we could re-visit the stretch"

In spite of the fact that I felt all the air had been sucked from the room, I politely asked him to make a copy of the reports he was holding so I could take them with me to Dr. Mac.

Once the doctor departed, Katherine stood in front of me and quietly said, "D, you're turning white. Just breathe. This will all be resolved. Right now just stay as calm as you can."

Staring into her eyes, I followed her masterful instruction. We collected the large manila envelope with the report from hell in it, and we left.

Once we were outside, I immediately placed a call to Dr. Mac's office, only to learn he was on vacation for the next two weeks. Since I couldn't reach him I called Tessa and asked her what to do next.

Tessa encouraged me to make an appointment with Dr. Deschler, who was the head of the department where I was being treated at Mass Eye and Ear. She considered him to be the best specialist to perform this procedure. However, Dr. Deschler was in high demand. Tessa said she would help me get the appointment under one condition: if Dr. Deschler determined a neck dissection was necessary, I had to agree.

Time to pray:

Dear God, I place my hands in your hands. Help me to hold this decision like a flower, like a bird whose wounded wing needs love. Breathe me into this decision with love. Let love guide me.

Whatever I decide I know you are blessing me with a complete and total healing. Should I choose surgery, by the grace of God, I will have an easy time of it. Let this all unfold gracefully.

The next day was a punky feel'n kinda day. I was in a contemplative mood so I decided to paint all day. I needed time to be immersed in the creative process. It didn't matter much what the canvas looked like. The process was more important. Time stood still and sat on a shelf like an old rusty clock when I was lost in a painting. Hours passed and would seem like minutes.

Stepping back from a painting at the many stages of the process taught me to apply the same lesson to other aspects of my life. I stepped back often. I wanted to get a clearer view of my life's canvas just as I did my artistic canvas.

That day, I also went for a walk, solo. Not so long ago, a five mile walk in an hour was routine. Now, I was thrilled when I made it to the corner and back.

***

Dr. Deschler was a soft spoken, compassionate man with small framed glasses, sandy colored hair, and an Ivy League studiousness.

I felt I was in extremely capable hands. He was a smaller framed man but he possessed a huge presence. The entire Dream Team fell in love with him. According to him, there was no need for another PET scan. He studied the results of the scan prior to the appointment and concurred with the folks in Salem that a neck dissection was necessary.

He also wanted a biopsy of the tongue where the scan had showed some activity. During the visit he asked, "Which is your dominant hand?" My right being my dominant he asked for my left arm. As he stretched my arm, he squeezed my wrist and held it for about thirty seconds. While he performed this task, the fingers of his opposite hand poked at my forearm.

Marsha and I were puzzled. Then he asked, "Do you want to know why I am doing this?" Yes I do.

Then he unloaded. "If the biopsy shows any sign of cancer I will need to remove the back of your tongue. I will perform both the neck dissection and the removal and rebuilding of your tongue at the same time, and I will use the skin of your forearm, a vein, and an artery to re-build it."

The walls once again moved closer and sucked up every bit of available air. I tried not to vomit. The imminent neck dissection now somewhat paled in comparison to the thought of him removing my tongue.

Once again Marsha and I rode home in deafening silence. As I opened the car door, Marsha said, "Mona, there is no way in hell they're taking your tongue off."

I whispered, "I know my friend...I know."

Marsha was right. Should that have been the case, I would not have allowed them to remove the back of my tongue and destroy my arm in the process of rebuilding another part of me.

The doctors had already warned me I would never be able to eat normally after such extreme radiation. And I might not be able to sing the way I had sung in the past. As it was I couldn't eek out a single note. I hated the feeling of not being able to sing. I prayed daily for my voice to return to normal.

If they had to reconstruct my tongue the possibility of singing would be diminished even further. At that point I had to release any attachment I had to the outcome. I could only pray the results would be in my favor so I would not be faced with such a decision.

I know I made a deal with Tessa that I would do what Dr. Deschler said regarding the neck dissection, but it would take time for me to make my own decision.

Dr. Deschler recommended that I wait to perform the surgical stretch on my esophagus. He was concerned the tissue was still too compromised, and the risk of perforating my esophagus was too great.

I told him, "The only way I will consent to having the biopsy is if you perform both surgeries at the same time, the biopsy and the stretch." He must have read by the look in my eyes that I was unwilling to give an inch. Dr. Deschler agreed to do both surgeries at the same time. I think he thought I drove a hard bargain. Sometimes I did.

What he didn't know was what had transpired during my last shamanic healing session with Marc.

In that last healing session Jesus' energy had been prominent. Jesus had stood at the foot of my bed and His hands turned to pure light. I opened my mouth and felt the light reach through my mouth and into my throat. Marc said he could actually see the light filling my throat and chest area. After which I heard the words…"You are healed."

If I had shared that experience with Dr. Deschler, it could have diluted the sacredness. At that time I could not handle any skepticism. I claimed my knowing. That moment in the Presence had given me the confidence to take the stand that the surgical stretch would be a success.

The next few days I felt awful. My digestion and intestines were symphonic. I had made an abnormal number of visits to the bathroom which prompted Marsha to ask,

"Mona, you doing okay?"

I dragged myself back to my recliner and said, "I don't think so."

I felt so sick. I couldn't keep anything in my stomach. As fast as the food traveled through the tube and into my stomach, I headed to the bathroom. After three days of this exhausting intestinal commotion, I called the doctor.

I had to get a stool sample to the hospital for testing. Within hours, the doctor's office called to report I had a very serious condition called clostridium difficile, more commonly known as C-diff. C-diff is a bacterium that could cause life-threatening inflammation of the colon. It was most commonly found in elderly people or people who had been hospitalized. The doctor believed I contracted it during one of my visits to the hospital.

Treatment was nasty. I began taking an anti-fungal called Flagyl, a highly toxic drug. I had no choice but to take it.

My already compromised immune system couldn't handle the serious assault the C-diff had on my body and the doctors worried that it could develop into something life-threatening. As long as this ran rampant in my system, there was no way I could have the stretch.

I could not be admitted to a hospital with a contagious condition, nor could my system tolerate the additional stress of surgery.

I had heard several people say, "It isn't the cancer that kills you it's the treatment." I began to understand what they meant.

I did my best to remain optimistic. All I wanted was to get my esophagus stretched but stuff just kept happening. I felt depleted. I didn't want to give up but I was sliding down a slippery slope.

A few weeks passed and the C-diff seemed to be under control. We headed to the hospital for the long-awaited biopsy and stretch.

The importance of the biopsy could not be under estimated, but my eye was on the prize and the prize was stretching my esophagus.

The routine garb, the ceremonial signing of appropriate papers, different nurses and doctors asked the same questions. It all took place in a timely fashion. We awaited Dr. Deschler's arrival. Once he arrived, he slipped himself into the small space between the curtain and the rail of my gurney, and asked with his sparkly smile, "How are we today?"

To which I replied, "I'm doing okay, a little anxious, but I'll be asleep soon and it won't matter."

He chuckled, instructed the nurse to administer the beginning stage of sedation, and within moments I didn't care about being wheeled in for surgery.

I awoke in recovery to the sweet faces of Deleta and Marsha. Smiles galore! Dr. Deschler called them immediately after surgery with a great report. He would visit me in recovery as soon as he was finished in surgery.

I loved hearing the good news, but the pain I felt was excruciating. The biopsy was more extensive than expected. In order to get good margins, he had to remove a good size chunk of the back right corner of my tongue and a small portion of the inside of my cheek where my tongue and cheek met.

Damn that hurt!

Dr. Deschler bounced across the room, stopped dead in his tracks at the foot of my bed, and lit up the room with an ear to ear grin. It was more than just a smile. It was a face filled with all the joy he could muster. With childlike giddiness he said, "What a fabulous stretch. It could not have been more perfect. I was able to stretch to twenty eight centimeters which is remarkable. And, the biopsy went well. I apologize for the extensiveness but I wanted to make sure we got good margins and a clear picture."

I quietly whispered, "Thank you Jesus."

I told the good doctor I understood and expressed my appreciation for honoring my request to perform the stretch. I contemplated telling him the Jesus story, but wasn't sure he would understand. I was happy it was over and I nervously awaited the results of the biopsy.

As I grew stronger, and was able to talk better, friends would visit for longer periods of time. Jean came over to visit and we decided to create our own shamanic journey. We used drums, rattles, and the sound of our own voices in chant. My ability to chant was limited so I quietly hummed.

A shamanic journey was a way of finding answers, information, healing, wisdom and knowledge as well as guidance. During the journey you meet spirits who may be regarded as ancestors, elders, gods, goddesses, spirit guides, and power animals. These beings are seen as providers of great wisdom, power, and the ones who are willing to help with guiding the living.

Jean rattled and I drummed. I could sense a Native American Indian energy had poured into the room. After we drummed we fell into silence for about twenty minutes. During the silence, I felt the presence of a tribal woman. I sensed her image. She had long white clothing that draped her small frame, long feathered earrings, and a young beautiful face. I felt her take my face into her hands, turned my head and began to blow smoke into the left side of my neck. Then she led me over a knoll where hundreds of Buffalo ran. We went down into the valley where tribal people of all ages were standing in a circle. She laid me down in the center and the tribal people sprinkled me with dirt. It felt like I was being blessed. She sat at my head and blew smoke over me and caressed my forehead. I knew I wasn't dreaming because I wasn't sleeping. This was as real as when the Blessed Mother appeared during meditation at Shaman class.

After Jean left, I looked up Buffalo medicine in my Animal Medicine book. Buffalo medicine was about Prayer and Abundance and "White Buffalo Calf Woman" was the one who brought the sacred pipe to the people of the Lakota tradition and taught them to pray. The smoke was considered to be visual prayer and was very sacred and cleansing. Until that evening I had no knowledge of Buffalo medicine or White Buffalo Calf Woman.

The next day I visited Dr. Savastio at the naturopathic health clinic. He was always excited to see me but today he was more excited than usual. He couldn't wait to share what he and his wife had done over the weekend.

They had traveled to Canada and participated in a ceremony for his friend who had died last year. His friend was a Lakota Indian and on the first anniversary of their death, loved ones gather, share smoke and honor the person's spirit by weeping into a white cloth, and then they use their tears to cleanse themselves.

I shared with him my experience from the previous evening. He was familiar with the story of White Buffalo Calf Woman from his Lakota friend. The two of us were stirred by the serendipitous and synchronistic events.

Two days after my visit with Dr. S. I went to my friend Marty for a healing session. He was someone I had seen on and off for several years.

During the treatment, he took tissues and placed them on my neck, and blew into the left side of my neck. He had never done that to me before. Afterwards I asked him if that was something he had been incorporating into his healing work.

He said, "No, in the twenty plus years I have been practicing, I may have done something like that once or twice."

Unaware of the past week's events, he offered me a gift. He handed me a beautiful ceramic bowl and said, "I think this belongs to you." It was a burnt sienna colored bowl with a Buffalo painted on it. I immediately took the bowl and unhesitatingly I began to softly humming Native American sounds into the bowl.

The sounds that came from me were subtle but extremely powerful. I asked him what this bowl was intended for and he said "It's a planter." We both laughed hysterically and I chortled, "Not any longer."

Each experience had been transformative, each one built upon the other. They had created a synergy and strong foundation for self healing.

I believe transformative experiences like these are available to each of us so long as we remain open and welcome the assistance from beyond what meets the eye.

I was happy I had.

Approaching the finish line   Marsha and Me

Denise's Dream Team

Hugging Deleta at the finish line

The PMC starting line   PMC finish line, Deleta,
                                 Marsha, Me, Diane & Johnny

PMC 2005

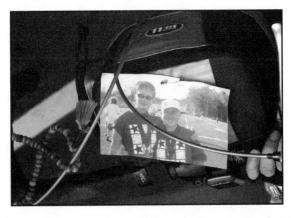

The photo of Karen and me that carried me to the finish line

Full moon fire ceremony

Harvesting the grapes in Paciano, Italy

At my villa in Italy

 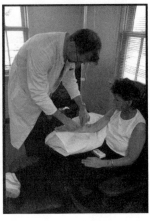

Healing from the
neck dissection

IV nutrients administered
by Dr. Savastio

The dreaded mask

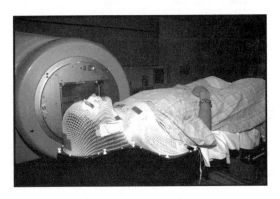

The monster machine

Larry Lucchino and I hugging

The moment of ordination

Rev. Denise

One year old

Sitting with Ed
(Santa) at my 50th

Laughing at my
50th with Tim

Karen and I at the Relay for Life

Showing off my scar

Singing at Fenway

Twelve

It's Time to Make a Decision

"You DO know what to do."

- Louise Hay

My best buddy, Marsha, and I were in the waiting room at my gynecologist's office, waiting for me to be called in for my annual checkup, when I felt the urge to check voicemail on my home phone. Ignoring the signs that said…Please turn off all cell phones, I placed the call.

The computerized voice announced, "You have one new message." My silent prayer, "Please let it be Dr. Deschler." The mere sound of his voice caused a slight blip in my breathing. "It's Dr. Deschler, the tongue biopsy is benign. That's really good news. See you in my office. Take care."

I listened to the message. I didn't smile. I didn't cry. I simply hit the replay button, placed the phone against Marsha's ear and watched her face light up. Her eyes mirrored mine as both of us filled with tears. We embraced, and I sobbed. I melted into my friends arms, relieved. While Marsha held me close I released an exhale from the low register of my lungs. A place I had not been able to access easily while I waited a week for that call.

A few moments later the nurse opened the door to the doctor's offices and announced my name. I unwrapped myself from Marsha's embrace and headed toward the door.

"Are you okay?" The nurse asked.

"I am more than okay. I am ecstatic." On our way down the hall I gave her the update of my latest news. We almost skipped to the appropriate office.

Marsha and I had to suppress our excitement in the lobby of the doctor's office so once outside I phoned my sister, Deleta, to share the good news. I pushed the "speaker phone" button so the Dream Team could whoop it up and celebrate together.

Although the news was magnificent, my tongue still hurt. There was quite a hole at the biopsy site. I kept a close eye on the healing process with my nifty little flashlight that illuminated the layers of tissue below the surface. In a strange sort of way, it fascinated me to be able to view the construction of my body.

According to Dr. Deschler, the reason for the severe pain and slow healing was because of the destruction the radiation caused to the tissue. I no longer had the necessary bacteria to help heal the incision. It would take four to six weeks for me to heal. The stretch was intended to help me eat, but I could not eat until the site mended.

The egregious greed of the insurance industry astounded me. Next month would be my last month on short-term disability. And I had already been denied long-term disability.

This halted my only source of income, which added a mountain of stress to an already emotionally taxing situation. I had to put this all into perspective and make a decision regarding the neck dissection.

I agreed I would do what Dr. Deschler suggested. And he did make it clear surgery was necessary, but having to stay true to my commitment to Tessa to move forward with surgery would delay my return to work. Without disability, I could not possibly afford to extend my unemployed status for another three to four months.

The temerity of the industry repulsed me. Their concerns were focused on profit, not on how to provide for a policy holder in dire straits. According to them, my disability coverage had not yet begun when I went for the initial biopsy, so my condition was considered pre-existing, and therefore not covered. They have mastered the art of weaving loop holes in their favor.

I was pissed off, fed up, and disappointed. I reunited with my anger management tool, the wiffle ball bat, and emancipated myself from all the negative, hostile emotions. I felt, expressed and released the destructive feelings and then let it all go. Had I stored them I would have interfered with my healing process. And healing was my priority.

At that time I was single and felt lonely which added to my emotional roller coaster. I knew I was so loved and supported by so many wonderful people but I missed having a primary relationship. I was facing a major decision and it would have comforted me to have a partner to discuss the pros and cons, and the "what ifs."

I looked forward to a having a healthy partnership but now many people would consider me to be a high risk person to date because I had had cancer. In addition I had to face the fact that a neck dissection would be disfiguring. How much harder would it be to find someone who would accept me?

Being attractive enough to date was no reason to have the surgery or not have the surgery, but part of that decision was accepting the fact I was going to be disfigured for life. I wished I could lay my weary head down, fall asleep, and awake to knowing exactly what to do.

I was so tired of sleeping alone night after night. I longed to be held, both physically and emotionally. I had to acknowledge the feelings but knew it wasn't the time to grapple with them.

Even though I longed to be held, I recognized I was being held in the hearts of many.

Treatments at the clinic had been extensive and expensive. When I went for my next treatments the hyperbaric chamber was first on the list, then I had a colonic, and the day ended with an acupuncture treatment. When it was time to check out, I reached for my checkbook, and the front desk attendant said, "No charge today. Someone anonymously deposited one thousand dollars into your account."

Although I heard the word, "anonymously" I still asked, "Who?"

She said, "They asked me not to tell you and I need to honor my word." I burst into tears.

If I decided to move ahead with the neck dissection, I would need to continue to strengthen my immune system. This was critical. This gift insured at least another round and added elasticity to the money I had raised from the CD fund-raising effort.

A CarePages update:

Hello all you beautiful souls.

I went for a few alternative treatments today. Taking out my checkbook to pay, the attendant at the front desk told me someone had gifted me one thousand dollars, which was being held on account for me for future treatments. I cried all the way home at the enormity of your love and support.

I don't know who you are but I know you are reading this page right now. I would like to know who you are so I could personally thank you, but I respect your wanting to remain anonymous. Thank you from the bottom of my heart. Thank you to each and every person helping lighten the load. Because of your love and support I am preparing myself for the possibility of surgery from a very peaceful place within. Making the decision for such a major surgery is taking time. I will know when I know, and at this moment it is still unclear.

God bless each of you. May all your generosity multiply one hundred fold for you in health, prosperity, love, and peace. I am grateful. I wish I could put into words one tenth of what I feel. It just isn't possible.

Healthfully yours,
Denise

From then on, I looked at being denied long term disability as an invitation to rely on my faith more than ever. My head spun trying to figure out how I would go through surgery, stay on top of bills, and how I would survive emotionally. I did not question my faith; I questioned what the situation begged: "Where had I placed my faith? Had I placed it in the material world? In institutions? In money? Or had I placed my faith in the invisible but real gifts of spirit? I resorted to prayer and it provided the answer.

For a few days my prayers had been shallow and pointed because I had been in fear and couldn't get the emotional internal elevator moving the nine inches from my head to my heart. I knew I had to pray with conviction, commitment, and gratitude in advance for the manifestation of my prayer.

I released my fear the best I could and prayed without holding back. I realized money was not my source of all that was good. Institutions were not my source. God was and would always be my source. I relinquished concern about money and trusted my faith and placed my faith in trust.

This shift caused a miracle.

A spiritual practice I had adhered to for several years was tithing. The concept of tithing can be traced back to the Old Testament. In fact, the earliest instances of tithing can be found among Jews who required their citizens to pay a ten percent tax. There were many references to tithing throughout both the Old and New Testaments; one of the most specific could be found in the Book of Genesis where it said: "This stone, that I had set up as a pillar would be God's house, and of all that you give me I would give you a tenth" (Gen. 28:22).

In the truest sense, tithing involved giving the first ten percent of income - as opposed to giving whatever income you may have left over. In that manner, according to Scripture, you were assured that you were giving your very best.

Unity was where I had tithed because Unity was where I had been spiritually nourished. Over the many years of tithing miracles had occurred in my life but not to the magnitude of the miracle that had occurred that week.

For me, I understood tithing encompassed everything in life, and was not specific to money. If I wanted more love, give love away. If I wanted more compassion, give compassion. If I wanted more understanding, give understanding and so on. If I wanted more money, give some away.

That week I had given a friend one hundred dollars because they had been struggling financially. The gift I bestowed on them came after I had been denied my claim for long-term disability. Even though my stress level around finances had escalated, I chose to step out on faith and gave my friend the money. I knew the most propitious action to take would be to help someone else. I wanted to help my friend shift the energy around lack; all the while I trusted God to help us both.

A few days later I felt strong enough to attend the Wednesday evening service at Unity. Purposely, I left my checkbook and wallet home. I got into my car, started it, and went to put the car in drive when I heard a little voice say, "Not the time to hold tight. Now more than ever is the time to tithe." I got out of the car, retrieved my checkbook, and wrote a fifty dollar tithe and headed to Unity.

My friend Maryanne and I entered the church at the same time. We embraced for an extra special amount of time because we were so excited to see each other.

Maryanne is a delightful woman. She is 14 years my senior and has a "big sister" kind of love for me and I simply adored her. She was a very successful entrepreneur and had owned a thriving business for over 20 years, had a heart as big as Texas and an insight that had always offered me much consolation. I trusted her perspective.

After we hugged and had a short conversation, she told me she had something to discuss with me. Once service ended we folded ourselves into the comfy chairs at the back of the sanctuary when she said, "I have something to tell you and I just want you to listen. Please don't interrupt me. I have made a decision about something and there is no room for discussion or rebuttal."

I wasn't sure what she meant but I said, "Agreed."

Maryanne continued, "I heard about your news that you have been denied long-term disability. How could you possibly go through what you are going through, looking surgery in the face, with a stressful financial situation? You need to clear all that from the table and focus on what is important. I am going to gift the money you need to pay your bills for the next four months."

Even though I agreed to be quiet and listen, I immediately said, "No, I cannot let…"

Before I had a chance to finish my sentence she said, "Uh…uh…uh…I told you there is no room for discussion. I am gifting this money and you are accepting it."

I did what I had been doing a lot of those days, I cried at how blessed I was by the angels that kept appearing in my life.

I wrapped a tight arm around her neck and sobbed. Maryanne was an angel clothed as a woman.

For the first time in weeks I actually took a deep breath. I thought my asthma had been the reason for my struggle to breathe but it had been anxiety and stress that kept me from breathing deeply. The major obstacle had been removed, and my path to make the right decision about surgery had been cleared.

Over the next few days meditation helped me gain the insight I needed to arrive at the right decision. During today's meditation While Buffalo Calf Woman's energy drifted in. The image of her was the same as the first time. I saw myself in the midst of the tribe. They were burying my entire body in mud, except for my face. I understood this to be some type of ritual for keeping me safe. I heard the words, where ever these words, feeling, knowing came from. I got the message that, by all appearances, Dr. Deschler and the medical team at Mass Eye and Ear would be doing the surgery and they would not be alone. The healing energies of the tribe would fill the operating room and staff with light, love, perfection, and protection. The surgery was part of the plan to keep me safe from any future complications from cancer. I was not to be afraid.

In a conversation with my friend Hortensia about whether or not to have the neck dissection, I shared with her what I had seen in my meditation. She could not believe what she was hearing.

Hortensia shared a story with me that her aunt had told her of a time when her aunt was a young girl in Cuba. Her aunt could not walk very well and as she grew older her disability got worse. They suspected it was polio but in the early 1930's in Cuba there was not much they could do about polio.

Desperate to help her daughter walk, Hortensia's grandmother took her aunt to the local shamans/faith healers to see what they could do to help her. They buried her in mud for twenty four hours except for her face.

Of course, before Hortensia could even finish the story I asked, "What happened when they removed her."

Hortensia smiled at me and said, "She began to walk with a slight limp which is how she has walked her entire life."

Although the thought of a four and a half hour surgery was daunting, I needed to transcend the fear of letting them remove 35 nodes, the main muscle on the left side; the SCM muscle, my external jugular vein, and all the glands underneath my jaw. I made the decision to have the neck dissection.

I trusted the healing magnitude of the universe and did not hedge. I moved forward with conviction and determination and accepted the next phase of this journey as an important step in my mental, emotional, physical, and spiritual evolution. The fear around this situation was normal, but I could not let it overrule the sensible side of me that knew this was the right thing to do. Obviously the universe was leaning in my favor.

Time to pray:

Lord, my essence and energy within and all around me has cleared a path to perfect health. I feel free from any fear, discomfort, and unnecessary suffering. My body is a holy temple filling with the light of God, set ablaze by the Holy Spirit. I thank God for clarity of mind and purity of heart as I move toward the next phase of healing.

My entire body is relaxing and preparing for all the good you have for me.

I accept this goodness now.

So be it, so it is.

The next morning I made the long anticipated call to Dr. Deschler's office to schedule my surgery.

I went for all the necessary pre-op appointments, and surgery was set for the beginning of the following week.

Again, my spirituality had to allow for my personality. Although I knew that surgery was the next best step, every time I thought about the actual day of surgery, my body shook and my eyes involuntarily closed and I attempted to shut out the scary images of what that surgery might look like.

At the pre-op appointments I was briefed as to what I could expect post surgery. I would have to remain in the hospital for four to six days. Mass Eye and Ear Infirmary seemed to be the Ritz Carlton of hospitals. Forty two beds comprised the entire hospital. Dr. Deschler's office was only fifty steps from where I would be. Because of the intricate surgeries performed there, the nursing staff was highly trained and there were two nurses to each patient.

This was great news but after my stay at Salem Hospital, I insisted a family member stay with me overnight. Especially the first night.

Deleta promised and I knew she would be spending the night with me.

Each passing day I felt more confident I had made the right decision, but as the day drew closer my eyes shut more often as I tried to shut out the scary images.

Surgery was scheduled for a Monday.

The weekend before there would be a drum and rattle making workshop offered at Unity. What perfect timing!

I had decided to participate to keep me centered on the spiritual aspects of my life. My stomach was rumbling but I attributed it to nerves. I felt much like I felt when I had C-diff and I was hopeful it was not a recurrence.

When I arrived at the workshop I was overwhelmed by the amazing amount of intriguing and exotic items that were available to us for creating our drums and rattles. There were buckets full of bones, skins, tortoise shells, leather, feathers, shells, beads, string, paint, glue, and all the necessary tools.

Each of us had what was referred to in the shamanic world as our own individual medicine. Shamanic medicine is a merging of the seen and the unseen; the conscious and the subconscious; and a harmonizing of the mind, body and spirit. It is a healing practice which integrates the natural and spirit world.

This creative process of making our own drum and rattle was a powerful approach to uncover and understand what we required in order to achieve balance and harmony at a soul level.

I loved being submerged in that energy just prior to surgery. I traveled through another portal to a deeper level of self healing.

The first day was drum making day. Zelda, the instructor, called me over to the end of the room. When I reached her I looked down. She stood on a huge piece of buffalo skin and asked, "Would you like to cut the skin for your drum?"

"Sure," I said. "What do I do?"

"Stand on a spot and use your body as a pendulum. This is a sacred process where you and the energy of the buffalo will find the appropriate spot. If your body leans backwards that is an indication that spot is not the right place to cut. Move, and see what your body does next. When you find a spot and your body begins to lean forward, that's the perfect spot."

"Wow…how cool is that?!"

After a few attempts I found the perfect spot. Zelda handed me beautiful, long thin sheers. I offered gratitude to the buffalo and began to cut the hide, feeling the connection between myself, the buffalo, White Buffalo Calf woman, and my tribe. Tears filled my eyes, streamed down my cheeks and fell to the floor seemingly blessing the skin.

I never knew the reason but I was the only participant allowed to cut her own skin. I returned to my designated spot, I laid the skin on the table in front of me and placed my hands on it. I said a prayer and asked for guidance in making the perfect drum.

Nothing was to be wasted during this sacred process. Every bit of skin, even the tiny circles removed to create the holes where the rawhide was to be strung, were saved. I placed them into a tiny red piece of cloth that I made into a medicine bag and I tied it to the back of the drum.

Making the drum kept getting disrupted by having to visit the ladies room every hour. Nervous about the bathroom trips, I placed a call to my doctor's office. It was Saturday so I had to deal with the on-call doctor. After I explained my symptoms and my history of C-diff, she called in a prescription.

Surgery was only two days away and I couldn't take any chances. I picked up the prescription at lunch time, and by the end of the day the rock and roll band in my intestines had ended their tour.

By the close of the workshop, my drum was tight, beautiful, and the deep resonant sound penetrated me to the core. My creative juices stirred just thinking about the following day's rattle making workshop.

I couldn't wait for the walk-about process of choosing our special items.

I spent that evening getting to know my drum. I sat and tapped lightly on the skin. Then I held it above my head, with the skin toward me, and I tapped it with the mallet and felt its sound spill over me. The skin was tight, the sound was deep and the construction was strong. It reflected what I felt.

The next day Zelda suggested we be fully engaged and to take our time to choose our materials. Rattle medicine was important medicine for our individual healing, and our rattle would be something that would be with us as a healing tool throughout the rest of our lives. The process was sacred and was not to be taken lightly.

My savior, Maryanne, decided to participate in the workshop. Sharing this sacred experience with her brought us even closer.

I chose a small bone, a turtle shell, and several beads for the inside materials for my rattle and deer skin for the covering. Zelda asked, "Why did you choose that particular bone."

I told her, "No particular reason. It just called to me."

"I have had that bone in my possession for many years. I always knew that some day it would end up with the perfect person. It is a special peacock bone and peacock medicine is all about confidence."

I had not known what peacock medicine was about but throughout my life I had always loved peacocks. My friend Julie had given me a beautiful, hand-painted peacock that stood two foot high. I had always kept it within sight.

This entire process had helped me build my confidence that I could endure the impending surgery. And the peacock bone as the handle of my rattle helped me to handle the situation with more ease and grace.

In that moment I wondered how the staff at Mass Eye and Ear would have responded if I had shown up for surgery with my rattle?

Imagine if alternative medicine and traditional medicine could coalesce, creating an environment where patients could feel safe requesting exactly what they needed while they explored the many different paths to healing. Hopefully some day showing up with drums and rattles would not seem so far-fetched.

I spent the night before surgery with my drum and my rattle. I would drum for a while and feel its voice pulsing through me. I had filled my rattle with several beads, and its sound was dense and rich. As the beads hit against the sides of the turtle shell I could feel the richness penetrating me. I knew this was only the beginning of two beautiful friendships.

Surgery day. I was confident I had made the right decision.

Unfortunately, the Dream Team was minus one. Marsha was on vacation in St. Maarten. Her trip had been planned long before my surgery had been scheduled. As much as she hated being away, she had no choice.

That morning, Tim, and Julie, drove me into to Mass Eye and Ear. As we approached the valet parking directly in front of the hospital, on the other side of the lobby glass, I saw a very solemn looking Deleta, with Kelly standing beside her with her arm around her mom.

I had taken an Ativan that morning and felt pretty calm.

We all rode the elevator to the surgical wing on the fifth floor. By this time the drill was second nature so I fell into step immediately.

Once in my robe and footsies, I waited in the waiting room with my tribe.

The elevated television screen in the far corner of the room had captured everyone's nervous attention. This was a good distraction. But the distraction didn't replace the anxiety each of us experienced while we waited for the hand off from my support team to the surgical staff.

The abrupt noise from the jolt of the door behind the nurses' station startled me, and a familiar looking nurse announced my name. Smiling she said, "Hi honey, time to come with me." Despite the Ativan I still felt the pounding of my heart pulsing in my ears.

With misty eyes each of us embraced. They sent me off with "I love yous" and words of encouragement to be strong. My sister's embrace was particularly strong and lasted longer than the others. The way she held me, let me know I was safe. And beyond a shadow of a doubt, we would see each other on the other side of surgery.

There were no gurneys to transport me from the fifth floor to the surgical unit in the basement, so a nurse, an orderly, and I boarded the elevator on foot and headed down to surgery.

All the necessary electrical pads were stuck on my arms, chest and back. A pleasant nurse approached with the all too familiar red box to implant the IV. She performed her task without a glitch, and as she left she wished me luck.

For the next forty five minutes several doctors, nurses, and orderlies visited, all asked the same questions "What is your name? What is your date of birth? What are you having done? Who is the doctor performing surgery?" They wanted to make sure there were no mistakes and that they had the right girl.

The assisting physician reviewed my chart and he noticed the information about C-diff and asked, "How are you feeling?"

"I feel okay." And I updated him about how I had felt over the past weekend and that they had prescribed more medicine. He asked me if I had had a series of three consecutive stool samples which would had to have taken place in a three-day period to determine if I was clear of being contagious. This would also have eliminated any risk to me personally. At that point I said, "I have no idea what you are talking about."

He lightly patted my right thigh, smiled and said, "I'll be right back."

When he returned he had another doctor with him and a nurse. They came to inform me that it was not possible for them to operate on me because I could be in danger with having C-diff in my system. The risk was far too great.

Surgery was postponed for two weeks while I followed a rigorous protocol of more Flagyl.

The nurse came and removed the wires that had been strategically placed and the intravenous that had been so smoothly inserted.

The juxtaposition of relief and disappointment overwhelmed me. This turn of events was just too bizarre. What the hell is this all about?

I lay there and waited to be brought back upstairs and thought; *is this some kind of sign? Why am I not supposed to have surgery today? Was all the preparation and anguish for nothing? Is today not the best day? Or is no day the best day?*

I had spent all that time deliberating endlessly, and in a moment the universe had shifted the energy dramatically. I felt as if I had been dropped from an airplane without a parachute. I was emotionally deflated. I couldn't wait to get home and pour myself into my recliner and sleep.

Deleta and Kelly were paged and told that surgery had been postponed and I would be discharged within the hour.

The emotional treadmill we had all been on getting prepared for that day exhausted us and didn't accomplish anything, which was a lesson in the futility of emotional stewing.

Deleta and Kelly had arrived and they looked more relieved than disappointed. I later learned why.

Before I was discharged, the nurse instructed me to call Dr. Deschler's office when I got home so they could re-schedule surgery. *We'll see.*

In that moment I didn't know the reason why I had to wallow in that waiting period, but with everything I had been through I had learned to accept reality more quickly. I knew all things worked for good, and everything in life was divinely guided. And when circumstances like that bubble up through the many layers of universal truth I had to trust the process. Reminded yet again, of the Buddhist teaching, "All suffering comes from resisting reality." Surgery was canceled. That was the reality. Resisting that reality would have caused me more suffering. I honored myself and kept my vibration high and did not want to create more stress. I adjusted and accepted what had happened.

There would always be a situation that would attempt to disturb my sacred vibration. Life happens. Living a spiritual life had its own unique rewards. It taught me to have patience when challenges appeared. I trusted there was a reason for the way this had all unfolded.

On the ride home Deleta and Kelly told me what had happened earlier in the day. Kelly said she believed that the universe had been in protective mode.

I learned that, after I had headed off to surgery with the nurse, Kelly's cell phone rang. It was Beth, Kelly's sister. Beth was panicked. She begged

Kelly not to let them operate on me. Beth pleaded with Kelly to find a way to stop the surgery. Speaking softly and calmly Kelly tried to soothe Beth's nerves by telling her that it would all be okay and I was fine.

Beth insisted it was not fine but she stopped begging because she knew there was nothing Kelly could do about halting the surgery. But the universe heard her plea.

Beth had seen a dead wolf on the side of the road on her way to work that morning. This was an upsetting sight in its own right and for Beth it was also an omen that had to do with me and surgery.

When she saw the wolf Beth recalled a story I had told her about a powerful experience I had had two years prior while having another surgery.

As I was preparing for that surgery, Marc called me the day before and suggested I call on Wolf and Raven medicine to assist me and protect me. To Native Americans the Wolf and the Raven were sacred. The Wolf was a powerful spiritual symbol. They were considered to be teachers and pathfinders. Wolf medicine was very ancient medicine. Wolf helps us begin cycles of experience and seek inner truth, and Raven was the messenger of magic from the great void where all knowledge waits for us. Their powerful medicine could give us the courage to enter the darkness of the void called the Great Mystery.

After speaking with Marc, I lowered myself into my meditation chair and began meditating when an undeniable image of Wolf and Raven appeared. Wolf was circling the operating room and Raven was perched in the center of the operating table. Wolf was slowly pacing the circumference of the room. This was also the last image I remembered as I fell asleep that evening. The morning of surgery I meditated again. Again, the exact same image appeared, Wolf slowly pacing and Raven perched.

On the way to the hospital, I shared my Wolf and Raven experience with Marsha.

When I arrived at Anna Jacques Hospital in Newburyport, MA I went through the appropriate routine and was then assigned a delightful nurse who had beautiful sky blue eyes and soft curly blonde hair. She had a sweet soft smile and a tender bedside manner.

Our communication was kept to a minimum by the busyness of the day. The surgery took only a few hours and was a success.

In recovery, I remembered searching for Wolf and Raven. Closing my eyes and calling them forth was to no avail. When Marsha arrived I told her I didn't feel Wolf and Raven's energy around me any longer. She suggested maybe it was because they did what they came to do and then went on their way.

At that moment my nurse checked in to see if I was stable enough to be discharged. Since I was still a bit groggy she decided it would be best to transport me out to the car in a wheelchair.

It was a bitter cold, February day so while she collected the wheelchair; she also removed a jacket from a hook in front of her. Facing in the opposite direction, she slid one arm into her jacket and then the other, as the jacket stretched across her back so did the majestic face of a wolf with piercing green eyes that stared directly at me.

I shuddered. Marsha gasped. Wide eyed, we stared at each other in disbelief. I looked at the nurse and stated the obvious, "There is a wolf's face on the back of your jacket."

She smiled and said, "There certainly is. I'm Wolf woman"

I said, "What do you mean… wolf woman?"

She told us that she adores wolves and over the past several years had adopted seven wolves. She spent most of her free time volunteering at a place a few towns away called Wolf Hollow. And she said, "If people learned how to live like wolves live, this world would be a much more beautiful and peaceful place."

Though her statement intrigued me, I didn't pursue that conversation. I chose not to share my wolf story with her either. I was too astounded.

It's surgery day and Beth sees the dead wolf on the side of the road. She is emotionally catapulted back to the story I told her from two years ago and my connection to wolf medicine.

For Beth, the wolf had been a glaring sign, that day was not the optimum day for me to be in surgery. Her demand the surgery be halted came from a purely connected place.

And…Marsha had been my wing woman through it all. It was difficult for her not to be with me for such a major event in my life.

A confluence of energies pleased everyone.

My only task was to trust the process, trust the knowing that the intelligence that coursed through everything that was right and perfect and good had been working diligently in my favor one hundred percent of the time. That intelligence had placed me on the right and perfect path that day.

No…that day was absolutely not the day for surgery and I was happy that I had been plucked from the surgical floor at Mass Eye and Ear Hospital.

Thirteen

This Time it's for Real

---

*"I know God will not give me more than I can handle.
I just wish he didn't trust me so much."*

- Mother Teresa of Calcutta

Surgery was re-scheduled for two weeks out.

During those weeks I took it easy and spent time with friends and family. I did what I had to do to heal from the C-diff and made certain there would be no chance of another cancelation.

Late one afternoon, I had a visit from my friend, Christine.

She and I had met several years before at Unity, and for the past eighteen months we had been prayer partners. Each morning at 7 a.m. we spoke and alternated days calling each other.

We would listen to each other's prayer request for that day, and affirmed the prayer back to each other. We carved out just five minutes each day, but often that five minutes were some of the most powerful minutes of my day. It bolstered the energy of our intention for the day and helped us remain mindful of what had been affirmed.

Our prayer time was interrupted only a few times due to my early morning medical appointments. When I had very little voice to affirm her prayer, I would pray silently and she swears those days were the most powerful for her. On those days I would keep my prayer to few words and somehow she would tune in and know exactly what I needed.

The afternoon visit turned into a toning and sounding healing session. We toned the different sounds of our chakras, and when the toning ended we slipped into a beautiful meditation. This was the third time we had done this and each time my voice grew stronger and clearer.

Christine shared the profundity of her experience, and said after the times we had met, she felt more balanced, more peaceful and more grounded for several days afterwards.

She asked if we could record one of our sessions so she would be able to work with the tones on her own. If I recorded it, it would help her remember the particular tones for each chakra because once she got home after our sessions, she had trouble remembering the sounds.

I knew once this surgery was over and I had been healed, my life would be used in a way to help others connect to their divine essence. I had no idea how it would all unfold. It was my business to know why I wanted something to happen and how it happened was God's business. Give me time to heal and then point me in the right direction.

Christine's request turned out to be the first step to my recording a sound healing CD, "Make a Joyful Noise" that has assisted people in learning about the power of sound healing and how to practice in the privacy of their own homes.

***

Death was also God's business, and God chose to usher my brother-in-law Bill home that week. As sad as it was for my sister Diane and her family, at least Bill had been relieved of the severe pain of lung cancer.

My heart ached for my sister and her family.

He was an extremely private man and didn't want any wake or funeral so she and her family opened her home to visitors.

When I went to pay my respects, Diane said, "I'll see you next week honey. I will wait and visit you the day after surgery."

I said, "Don't worry about coming to the hospital. You've been through enough." She hugged me and said softly, "I'll see you there."

Surgery was just a few days away and I was ready and I was also scared. Even though I had known the routine, I still felt scared when I thought about the intricacies and the seriousness of the surgery.

There was no doubt I was in the best hands, medically and spiritually. So many people prayed for me and held the high watch.

I read a quote that had inspired me: "Turn pain into purpose."

I knew I would turn all this pain into my purpose in life. I felt deeply grateful for the lesson I had learned, and I knew there were many more around the corner because that's how life works. I had been chosen to do this work as an expression of the Divine and as an example of how true healing was possible.

Round two!

The Flagyl had done the trick and all three stool samples returned negative. It was time.

I had decided to keep the crowd to a minimum this time so Marsha and I headed to Mass Eye and Ear. Deleta joined us there.

Marsha and Deleta were such a fabulous team. I had witnessed their love for each other and watched their relationship grow into a true sisterhood. The more we overcame the closer I saw them get. Throughout, they had kept their tears from me, but they must have used each others shoulders a time or two.

Deleta had arrived at the hospital before us and waited in the exact same spot behind the lobby glass. Each of us knew exactly where to go and exactly what to do, so we headed to the elevators, pushed the button for the 5th floor and took the ride in silence.

Again, the routine. For what I estimated to be the 150th time, I was donning my usual Johnny and footsies. The nurses had checked all the paperwork making sure everything was in order. Then it came time to say goodbye.

Marsha and Deleta had tears in their eyes as they wished me well and assured me they would be right there waiting for me.

Theirs was the hardest job. Every minute seems like an hour when you're waiting for a loved one to come through a serious surgery. Four and a half hours was a very long time. They knew, as I did, the risks of this surgery. Removing muscles, veins and nodes, severing nerves, and cutting through who knows what else could leave me unable to move my tongue and speak intelligibly. There was a chance my smile would be crooked, assuming I could smile at all on that side of my face. And most important of all, damage to the nerves of my larynx would leave me unable to sing.

My job was easy because for four hours I wouldn't have to think. I got to sleep through it all.

Once again, I was escorted through the heavy wooden doors to a room where I waited until they were ready for me in surgery. This time I got to ride on a gurney.

Once downstairs, all the necessary wires, needles, questions, and more questions were handled, and I was ready to go. Only this time I got to see Dr. Deschler.

He approached with that bright smile and asked, "Are you ready this time?"

I said, "Yes, but I have one request."

He leaned in and asked "What's that?"

"Would you take a moment and pray with me?"

I thought his eyes glistened as he said, "Absolutely."

We held hands and I said my standard default prayer, The Prayer of Protection. When I said "Amen," I felt him give a little squeeze and he walked beside me as they wheeled me into the operating room.

I had never seen an operating room quite like this one. It looked like the inside of a space ship. I remembered being transferred from the gurney onto the operating table, and before I drifted off, the last face I remembered seeing was Dr. Deschler's. I felt safe in his care. I would not have trusted any other doctor to perform such an intricate and invasive surgery on me. One tiny slip and I might be crippled in the most human ability there is, our ability to talk.

***

The minute I awoke The Dream Team was front and center. They never spoke about how scared they had been but they were sure glad to see me awake. Even though we knew I would wake up, with a surgery as serious as this one, there was always that outside chance that something could go wrong.

They looked relieved but also a little freaked out at the sight of me. The doctors had not bandaged my neck. One row of the thirty six staples that looked like railroad tracks began behind my left ear and ended just under my chin. The other row began at the mid-way point on my chin and made a vertical descent to my collar bone.

Even more painful to look at were the drains installed on either sides of my chest. Incisions just above both nipples had half inch tubes fed through them that traveled up to my neck to drain the fluid.

Once the nurses in recovery felt I could survive the trip, I was transported to my room which was directly across from the nurse's station. Deleta kept her promise and had her overnight bag in hand. She was not leaving her kid sister alone that night.

When the nurses realized she was intending to spend the night, they told her she couldn't stay. Groggily but forcefully I told them that my sister, would in fact, be staying with me for the night. She lived on Cape Cod and it was too far for her to travel that late at night and furthermore, I needed her beside me.

Although there was an extra bed in the room, my big sister spent the night in a chair at my side.

While I was in the hospital, the tag team of Kelly and Tim were assigned to update the CarePages.

Tim's first post:

Your humble correspondent Tim Hiltabiddle here – with an update on your friend and mine, Denise DeSimone. Good news. The doctors said that it went very well. She'll be out of post-op and in her room in an hour or two, at which point Deleta and Marsha will be able to tell us more.

I'll keep you posted.

Item of interest: On their way into Boston that morning, Denise and Marsha had to take a detour to I-93 because Rt. 1 in Saugus was closed due to flooding. Denise is in great spirits, however, and had a wonderful confidence and serenity in her voice, knowing that all is well and that today is the perfect day for her surgery. What a powerful example she is for us all.

Blessings,
Tim

Kelly's update later that same day:

Niece Kelly here with more good news from the halls of Mass Eye and Ear. Denise (Auntie Denise to me) is in her room and staying ahead of the pain with the help of some nifty drugs. (Who knows who she's running into on that Demerol-induced alternative plane of consciousness!)

Deleta (Mom) and Marsha are keeping a watchful eye and report that she looks great. The best news is that Denise passed the first functional/neurological test with flying colors – she could smile that gorgeous smile, purse her lips, move her tongue from side to side, and even lift her arm a bit! So, our favorite fierce little Italian is on the recuperation rampage!

Keep sending all those healing prayers – we know they are working!

Kelly's update on day two:

Hello all,

Denise is doing great. Deleta (Mom) camped out overnight with her to make sure she felt safe and comfy. Marsha spent the day there and sent Denise's big sis home for some rest.

Marsha reports that Denise has been out of bed and walking the room a few times today, including those all important trips to the bathroom that nurses are always so obsessed about. She's off the Demerol and on Percocet now, and she was talking pretty clearly in the background when this reporter was talking with Marsha. Marsha said Denise is in and out based on where she is in the Percocet schedule.

Let's hope she's timed things so she can watch her beloved American Idol tonight! Stay tuned for Tim's update tomorrow.

Kelly

Another update from Tim:

Another day of excellent progress for Denise. At the moment, I am told that, "She's sitting in a chair, her eyes were sparkly, her cheeks were pink, and she's smiling!" [thanks to Julie McConchie for that update] And there's reason to hope she'll be heading home within the next few days, so that's VERY good news.

Amesbury just hasn't been the same since she went to Boston, has it?! Dull, dreary, rainy and gloomy.

During my visit with her last evening we watched the semifinals of American Idol. Denise is still diggin' Elliot while I am down with Katherine, but we both agree that Taylor had the upper hand...but Denise thinks Taylor needs to stand up straight and stop crouching over and grimacing like he's constipated or something. Katherine sang well but if you ask me, NO ONE sings "Somewhere Over the Rainbow" as beautifully as our Denise.

Keep sending those prayers and good vibes; they are working wonders for her quick healing and fabulous attitude. And thanks to everyone who posted messages and sent emails and good wishes. I read them to her last night and she couldn't stop smiling!

Tim

What a great job Kelly and Tim did as they kept everyone up-to-date.

That hospital was way too uncomfortable and loud so when Dr. Deschler said I could leave the hospital when the drains were clear, I got to work and set a strong intention that the drains would perform their magic in record time.

Dr. Deschler and the staff couldn't believe I was well enough to be discharged after only three days.

Surprise! I wanted out and nothing was going to get in my way of being reunited with my recliner.

Kelly's day three, and final update:

Niece Kelly again, fresh from a nap after last night's wild slumber party in room 1129, with Great news tonight! The sun was out today, the birds were chirping their glorious sunset symphony, and former patient Denise (Auntie Denise to me) is HOME!!! Let's all pause and shout Yee-hah!

They removed the last surgical drain late this afternoon and sent her out into rush-hour traffic. After some slow going in the Marsha mobile, she's settling back into life in Amesbury and focusing on getting back up to speed.

Deleta (Mom) made a stop at Trader Joe's to get the makings for mango/banana protein smoothies and Denise will be back to her swallowing self in record time, especially if Deleta (Mom) has her way.

So now finally free from the 5 a.m. nursing staff hall cacophony, 6 a.m. vitals check, and frequent battles with hospital bed positioning and flat pillows, Denise can rest up in her freshly made comfy bed, put in some solid recliner time, get some reiki, go for walks, laugh with friends, commit a few scrabble homicides, and heal, heal, HEAL!

I'm sure the next update you read will be from the gorgeous (Auntie) Denise herself!

I had no recollection of the ride home from the hospital; I only remembered the happy tears I cried once Marsha got me in the house and settled.

I slept the entire night in my recliner, the only place I found comfortable.

The surgery had cut hundreds of nerves and the pain of even a light tee shirt felt as if five thousand volts of electricity had been pressed against my skin. I couldn't stand the pain of having anything touch my skin on the left side of my chest and neck.

I hadn't yet seen how my neck looked. I wanted someone with me. When the visiting nurse arrived the next morning we got out the mirror and I checked out my newly designed neck for the first time.

The incision was long, ugly, and painful with lots and lots of staples. Black bubbles of dried blood peeked through the incision. I looked like Frankenstein's bride.

The nurse reminded me that once the staples were removed the skin would relax. Over the next year the scar would smooth to a thin line.

I had to look straight because I could not turn my head. I used my left hand to keep my shirt away from my chest. I squeezed my eyes shut to block out the pain. It didn't work. I took long slow deep breaths. I prayed for the day the pain would subside.

Visits from my friends and family were my best medicine but I could only tolerate short visits.

Marsha had been my main care-taker since my return home. Her nursing skills had been honed to the point where no words were exchanged. Marsha always knew when to water me and hook me up to my feeding bag, Slim. I gave the name Slim to my vanilla colored Nutrin 101 and the pole it hung from. Slim was a good waiter.

The next day I sent out my first post-surgery update to my angels on the ground whose powerful prayers carried me through.

My first update post surgery:

Hi,

It's me…reporting from "The Recliner." Good to be out of the hospital and in my own home. Thanks to Kelly and Tim who so generously, eloquently and humorously kept you all up-to-date. What a team!!! You guys are quite talented.

I'm feeling as well as can be expected. Not a whole lot of energy so I am staying pretty close to the recliner. The walls in my home support me when I'm not clutching someone's arm. It will take a while to regain my strength. Thanks for all the love, support, prayers, and inspiring messages. I have said it before and I will say it again, "You are my medicine."

Next Friday I see the good doctor to have the staples removed. It will be two and a half weeks since surgery and I will be strong enough to head to Cape Cod to my sister's house for some much needed healing time.

Thank you God for my sister Deleta.

Many blessings,
Denise

FOURTEEN

Time to Heal

"I ask the great unseen healing force to remove all obstructions from my mind and body and restore me to perfect health. I ask this in all sincerity and honesty, and I will do my part. I ask the great unseen healing force to help both present and absent ones who are in need of help, and to restore them to perfect health. I put my trust in the love and power of God."

-Spiritualist Prayer for Healing

Two weeks later I was gazing out the 11th floor waiting room window of Mass Eye and Ear Hospital. It was just eight months ago when I looked out these windows for the first time, scared and confused.

That was last September when a team of doctors had told Deleta, Marsha and me, "If she doesn't move into treatment quickly, she may not be here for Christmas."

They had briefed us that day about my particular cancer. That was the first time I heard the words, "neck dissection."

That was the day I had seriously considered dying. I begged my family and friends to support me in my decision to never allow these doctors to dissect my neck.

Now eight months later on this day in May, I waited for Dr. Deschler to remove thirty six staples from where he had masterfully removed the left side of my neck. Is my lesson never say never? Maybe a more poignant lesson was that life is precious, and preserving life is what human beings do.

Eight months ago fear reared its head as a protective mechanism, and over time bowed its head to faith. Faith expanded and infused my life and proved to me the true protector is Divine guidance and the exquisiteness of the universe.

Lost in transcendental thought, I was startled as the nurse announced my name. I was immediately jolted back to reality.

Deleta and I rose from our chairs, followed the nurse, and sat in our regular seats.

When my personal miracle worker entered the room, much to my surprise and pleasure, Tessa was in tow. As Dr. Deschler poked around my neck Tessa exclaimed over and over, "This is amazing. You are doing so well. Most people are still in bed at this point."

Dr. Deschler took a few steps backwards, examined me, and said, "All done."

Giddily, I said, "All done…you mean all the staples are out?"

Earlier, when I had thought about the ceremonial staple removing I cringed at the thought of Dr. Deschler playing tug of war with my severely compromised neck. But the ceremony went off without a pinch

Another good lesson about why staying in the moment, and not lamenting future moments is a more peaceful way to live.

Dr. Deschler was pleased with my progress. So long as I remained quiet and got sufficient rest, he felt time on the Cape with family would be good medicine.

Memorial Day weekend at my sister's house was always a festive time. All twenty two members of her family were present, and the highlight of the weekend was Ryan's (Deleta's oldest grandchild) sixteenth birthday. I could swear that child was just christened.

The biggest hurdle I had to overcome during the weekend was the abdominal pain I had from laughing so hard. Each one of the children and grandchildren are amateur comics. All weekend they played off each other like actors in an improv theatre company. Their intelligent humor was refreshing

Once the family departed Deleta and I sat at the patio table and talked. I needed to share with someone whom I trusted. I needed to tell her some of what I had uncovered as I had explored the emotional underpinnings to my cancer. In my adult life I had prodded and explored and studied the unyielding traumas that had seeded themselves in my emotional and physical body. But the presence of cancer was the best present ever.

It goaded me and urged me to seek deeper levels of healing.

I was finished with being eaten up inside by anything or anyone. I was ready to love myself unconditionally. And it was important for me to share with someone I trusted.

Loving myself was my divine right, my birthright, and I was doing the work and wanted to claim my birthright once and for all.

Deleta had always been my champion. She, my brother John and sister-in-law Karen came to my aid when my father chose to disinherit me.

I was very close to my parents and visited them several times each week. For many years, I assumed my parents knew I was a lesbian. I had dated men throughout high school and beyond into my early twenties. From that time, fifteen years ago, until the "day of discovery" at age thirty five I had not dated men. I had lived with and been in relationships with women.

One evening while visiting my folks for dinner, the Oprah show was on in the kitchen. I arrived early and was awaiting my partner's arrival. I was chatting with my mom while she was cooking and my dad was perched at his usual, "head of the table" station. When the conversation quieted, I realized Oprah was highlighting Gay Pride week. As only Oprah could do she went directly to the heart of the matter with family members from both sides of the aisle.

There were several stories of people being disowned by their families.

I was so happy that hadn't happened to me. Nonchalantly I stated, "I'm so happy that you guys love me for who I am."

My father looked at me and said, "What do you mean?"

Thinking my dad hadn't been paying attention to what was on the television, I said, "It's Gay Pride week and Oprah is doing her show on the subject. I am happy you and Mom love me even though I'm in a relationship with a woman. There are people on this show who have been disowned by their families. And I'm glad you love me regardless."

My father's eyes began to squint, his brow furrowed, and he tilted his head to the side with his chin protruding as if to say, *What?*

On any given evening while my mother prepared dinner she was back and forth, and forth and back from refrigerator to the stove, stove to sink, etc. But suddenly my mother's feet appeared to be glued to the floor in front of the stove. She didn't move. She stared at the wall directly in front of her. She continually stirred the pot while the proverbial pot was being stirred by me.

She hadn't said a word so my father said, "I didn't know you were gay. Lillian, did you know your daughter was gay?"

My mother was spared having to answer by the fan fare which always accompanied my partner's grand entrance. "Hey DeSi! (her nickname for me for the past three years) Hey Lil! Hey Johnny!"

Without realizing the tension in the room, she walked over and ritualistically kissed my father in the middle of his forehead. After a few seconds she sensed the atmosphere was a bit hostile, she stopped talking, looked at me and said "What's going on Des?"

As if my parents were invisible, I delivered a blow-by-blow of what had transpired during the last twenty minutes.

Not another word was said. We turned off the Oprah show and ate dinner in silence. I was in shock. I was confused. I could not believe my father's reaction. How could he have not known?

Immediately upon finishing dinner my partner said goodbye, kissed my mother, avoided my father, glanced at me with raised eyebrows and said, "See you at home."

I cleaned up the kitchen and was about to leave when my father said: "Denise, you are my daughter and this is your home, but from now on she is not allowed in this home. You can visit any time you like, but you are to visit alone."

I didn't say a word, I hugged my mother and left.

I didn't tell my partner my father had chosen to ban her from his home. I was pleased that I never did.

The next morning my mother called to tell me that she and my father did not see eye to eye around the situation. After I left, she informed my father that I would be visiting with my partner, and if my father didn't like it, when we came to visit, he could go out.

When Deleta found out what had happened she went directly to my parents' home. I have always wished I had been a fly on the wall that evening.

According to my mother, Deleta arrived enraged. She didn't pull any punches. She told my father he was a hypocrite and a bully to treat his daughter that way. Deleta had a tender spot around this subject because she has a lesbian daughter.

Since he said nothing else over the next several months, I thought my father had softened around this issue. Then one day he called me into the backyard. That moment is embedded in my psyche. We were standing just outside to the left of the back door where the garden hose was coiled around its home. He could barely look at me.

He looked down at the worn out greenish hose. With a slight smirk, my father announced, "I've changed my mind about the house. I have decided to leave the home only to your sister Diane and rescind my offer for you to live here if you choose. You have no rights to any part of this home. The reason is because of the lifestyle you have chosen."

Thank God the hose was tightly coiled because as my insides coiled I wanted to grab that hose and blast him with it. Full force.

My father's choice to disinherit me was a clear message that to him I no longer counted. My being a lesbian discounted me as a person.

I never said anything about it or discussed it again. At the time I dealt with the pain and disappointment the best I could. I had been emotionally crushed by his decision and felt as if he had stabbed me directly in the heart. But it was easier to bury the hurt deep inside.

I later realized that, in order to truly forgive my father, I needed to dig in and detach the tentacles of suppressed feelings that sprouted from being emotionally abused.

My father didn't stop to think about the pain his decision would inflict. It crushed me that he thought there was something wrong with me.

And my life really didn't matter to him. He never said those exact words but, this was the message the child inside took away from the experience. And for many years I had unknowingly lived from the place that I really didn't matter.

In order to detach the tentacles of the feelings I had stuffed, I had to be brave enough to face all the feelings. And arrive at a place where I could forgive all.

It had taken twenty years, and a cancer diagnosis, and having to re-learn the simple function of swallowing to help make it easier to figuratively swallow and digest the truth about what had created blockages throughout my life.

These were the traumas David, Chun, and Marc referred to when they suggested digging deep in order to heal the wounds that needed to be healed, so I could give birth to a new me. A me who loved *me* unconditionally. It struck me that my navel was symbolic of my original birth, and the navel created by the scar from my feeding tube was symbolic of my rebirth.

I was relentless in my search to uncover the truth that helped me realize that I was not only my mother and father's child, I was a child of God. There was nothing I could do, had done, or would ever do, that would keep the love of my Mother/Father God from loving me. God loves me no matter what, and who was I to deny the object of God's love?

My father never reversed his decision to disinherit, but over time our relationship did improve. He too was a child of God. Who knows what demons from his past prompted him to react the way he did? I'm not a psychiatrist and I was not interested in trying to figure out what was going on for my father. In order for me to heal, I was interested in facing the truth of what had gone on for me.

Several years after our talk at the hose, my father was diagnosed with liver cancer. My partner and I visited him. He was now living alone. My mother had died a few years earlier. My dad missed her terribly. Whenever he would move from room-to-room, he carried a framed photo of her and kept it beside him.

It seemed he'd begun to realize the power of love, and that the commitment of love between two people was what mattered, not the gender.

That evening we said our goodbyes and as we approached the door with my partner in the lead, my father called to me, "Hey Denise."

I turned and said, "Ya Dad."

He quietly asked, "How did you get so lucky, finding a woman like her?"

I smiled and said, "Don't know Dad, but I'm glad I did."

Knowing he had a short time to live, it seemed to me that this was my father's way of telling me he had accepted me and that he loved me.

The night before my father's passing I was his care-giver. His weakness kept him from speaking but his eyes never quite left me.

By the time I had arrived the next day he had already been in a coma for several hours. My Aunt Mary (his sister) had been with him. The first thing my aunt said to me was, "Your father kept asking for you."

It troubled me to think my father had something to share that potentially could have been the salve that would have healed the wound that existed between us. But I had a good idea about what he may have said to me.

My father was sorry for his inability to fully accept who I was when he made those rash and ridiculous decisions and remarks about my sexuality. It was all there in his question, "How did you get so lucky?"

24 hours later, my father died in my arms.

***

Deleta and I finished our talk. I packed my things and got myself ready for the two hour ride home.

It was my first day home alone since my surgery. My alone time was my most precious time. Cable was out, so I had no internet or television and I was actually thankful there was no temptation of electronic distraction. Although the richness of that solitude had been rare over the past few months, I cherished it!

I anticipated many more days alone steeped in the process of re-creating me. I love the quote by George Bernard Shaw, "Life is not about finding yourself. Life is about creating yourself."

In the process of re-creating myself, I reflected on who I had been in the world. I had not always been my genuine, unique, authentic self. I was quick to anger. I also had an edge and a tone in my voice that had often sounded condescending.

I would act happy and content but often times I was bored with my life. I was trapped inside my own insecurities.

These trappings would surface in relationships. My inability to recognize these as insecurities would cause defensiveness and distance between me and others. My judgments of others created gaps between me and them. This caused me to ruminate on the negativity which destroyed my own happiness, not theirs.

As a child I had absorbed a lot of negativity and judgment by witnessing how my mother dealt with life. My Mom was a wonderful person with a big heart and a great sense of humor, but she would often fail to see the good in people.

She would focus on your faults, which often caused me to feel like I never did anything right.

Once I was grown, I would tease her about having, "Lil's Rule Book of Life."

I had never realized just how much of her energy I had absorbed and unconsciously duplicated in my own life, until I began to explore how much time I spent making people wrong for their behavior. I guess I too had created my own rule book of life.

Recognition and admission of my own inadequate behaviors, along with my willingness to jettison what did not serve my good, elevated me to an entirely new level of self healing and spirituality.

When I began the shift from being judgmental and became more curious, especially with regard to my own inner critic, it lifted a huge weight off my personality.

Being curious as opposed to being judgmental was fun. Even the word "curiosity" was softer and melodic. Judgment was abrupt. It severed my internal spirit and sharpened my already sharp edges even more. Cancer was instrumental in helping me smooth out the edges.

Curiosity opened a pathway for me to be more loving and kind. When I stepped even one inch from judgment toward curiosity it felt like a spiritual leap. The more I practiced shifting, the more quickly the shift would happen.

"Your soul has matured," Marc said during one of our last shaman classes.

He also said I was in graduate school of healing and that I needed to be physically still so I could journey deep spiritually. I needed time to process and integrate what I had experienced on all levels.

In the midst of my journey with cancer I had no time to hesitate or reflect. I anchored my rivets, made sure the ropes were tight, set my compass and kept climbing. In retrospect, the mountain I felt like I had climbed symbolized a sense of accomplishment and triumph.

As I reflected on the past few months, I was resolute that nothing would be too difficult for me to endure. I prayed for continued healing so I could use my life to make a difference and impact the world. I trusted God had the perfect plan for me, and it would unfold at the right and perfect time.

I needed to be patient and enjoy my healing time. In those moments, I enjoyed the view from my solitary tree house apartment. The flowers bloomed, the river banks out back were active with critters that were getting on with life, the peepers sang me to sleep, and the birds whistled me awake.

And I had plenty of time to watch my beloved Red Sox.

***

Tessa, my speech pathologist, was a Godsend. She was a fantastic coach, and I was coachable. I trusted her implicitly. She would set my mind at ease and give me great advice. She also gave me lots of homework which caused great angst. Her initial instruction a few months ago was to swallow a half cup of liquid within a half hour three times per day. It didn't sound daunting until I attempted it. It terrified me but I pushed on.

Now, in order for the doctors to agree to remove my feeding tube, I had to be able to swallow protein drinks and eat small amounts of soft foods.

Tessa helped me learn to eat again.

I ate yogurt, which initially caused painful tiny sores to break out all over my soft pallet. So I tried other foods like cottage cheese. Even the small curd kind was difficult to get down. Ice cream was soft but way too sweet. The best food to train with was baby food. My favorite was vegetable lasagna. At first, I managed to swallow a few teaspoons. Eventually I would eat one small jar of food within thirty minutes.

It was much easier to eat in the privacy of my own home than it was to eat in front of others. I felt nervous and would get embarrassed by having to eat so slowly and deliberately. I was too scared to talk while I ate, so socializing over dinner was a distant memory. I wanted the tube gone so I worked through my fear and swallowed.

One of the first times I ate in front of my family was the first weekend in June at a Relay for Life in Mansfield.

Several family members had gathered to support Johnny and Karen's children, who had worked tirelessly to organize their local Relay for Life event.

There was a buffet with a variety of foods. I honed in on the mashed potatoes and gravy because I knew I would be safe. No one spoke to me while I ate, they just smiled a lot.

Relay for Life events are sponsored by the American Cancer Society. They provide an opportunity to celebrate the lives of people who had encountered cancer. At Relay, teams of people camp out at a local high school, park, or fairground and take turns walking or running around a track or path.

Each team is asked to have a representative on the track at all times during the event. Because cancer never sleeps, Relays are overnight events up to twenty four hours in length.

The event always begins with a Survivors' Lap. The Survivors' Lap is an emotional time because it demonstrates that more lives are saved each year. It is also a time to recognize and celebrate the survivor's caregivers.

My CarePages Update after attending the Relay for Life

Hello,

I just returned from the Relay Walk for Life in Mansfield, MA. God bless Karen's children, my nieces and nephews and their spouses who all worked tirelessly to help make the Mansfield Relay a success.

They are determined to help find a cure to save their mother's life. It was wonderful to be with my family, especially Karen. With our eyes filled with tears and our hearts filled with love she and I walked the first lap, the survivor lap, together with other survivors and their caregivers. Karen, my brother John, and their children were in the lead. Mirroring the way it's been for the past eight months, Deleta was on my left and Marsha was on my right.

I was so proud to be a survivor

Thanks to all who contributed to the walk. Every bit helps. This particular walk set a goal of $145,000 and as of five o'clock today they had raised well over $200,000.

Please God let us see a cure for cancer in our lifetime.

Have a great weekend.

Love,
Denise

The weekend after the Relay for Life was my own personal Fourth of July. Regaining independence is an important step in the healing process for anyone who has suffered from a debilitating illness. For so many months I hadn't driven myself any where. I hadn't done my own laundry. Meal prep meant opening a can of vanilla flavored Nutrin 101 and hooking up the G-tube.

That weekend I drove myself to run a few errands and stopped to visit friends. Sitting at a red light, I checked the rear view mirror and I noticed I was smiling. For no apparent reason, I was just smiling. I was simply happy and it showed and glowed all over my face. Being out on my own did wonders for my soul.

Sunday of that same weekend was the first time I drove myself to service at Unity. They were minus one chaplain for the service so I stepped in to serve, which made my return even more blessed. My heart opened more with each passing moment among my spiritual family.

I was giving back to the people who had given so much to me over those past several months. The healer had been healed. This was an indication I was ready to go forth and do God's work. It was also an occasion when my spiritual community could witness my wellness after so many months of watching my illness.

Cancer had not defined me; it had re-designed me.

After an exciting weekend I settled in and prepared for the next day's colonoscopy. And the long-awaited removal of my feeding tube.

The most exciting CarePages update thus far:

Hello to all,

To say I am filled with emotion would be an understatement. My colonoscopy went very well. The results showed everything was clear. And the greatest news of all…are you ready??? They removed my feeding tube! It was inserted nine months ago this week; the perfect gestation period. I am reborn!

My sister Diane said, "You must felt like you lost a friend." That was exactly how I felt, so I packed it up and took it with me. I am going to have a ceremonial burial. It feels incredible to glance down and see my beautiful torso without an appendage. Now the raw area on my right side can heal from the months of having surgical tape stuck to it from holding the tube in place.

I have had a great week but I have also been a bit weepy. Grief from losing the left side of my neck snuck up on me and stirred lots of sadness. I always thought I would leave the planet with everything God granted me at entry. Grief is a natural and worthwhile feeling. Life is a series of deaths and rebirths, and grief is part of life and I know this. And I know it will take time to adjust.

I feel like so much of me has died (for the best) and the rebirth is tremendous. I am just now beginning to experience the effects of being reborn. More will be revealed in the book I am planning to write.

I am not the same person I was nine months ago. I am realizing the magnitude of the journey I have been on, and how God has a way of getting us through. At least me, anyway, giving me small doses at a time.

At first I was able to conquer the journey ten minutes at a time, then a few hours at a time, etc. Now, reflecting, I realize what I have been through. Looking back at the mountain I climbed in total awe.

A CarePages posting from my friend Hortensia said, "The climb will be easier if you take others with you." That is true. And my version is, "The climb WAS easier WHEN you take others with you."

I invited you, you joined me, and I could not have ever, ever done this without your love.

I will be closing the pages some time soon. I will miss the opportunity to connect but versions of the pages, and your wonderful messages will be in the book. Stay tuned.

My heart could not be more full.

I love you,
Denise

For the first time since my diagnosis I drove myself to the clinic for two treatments, the infrared sauna and acupuncture.

I spent time with Dr. Savastio, which was one of the highlights of the day. He was so proud of how much progress I had made and was so humble about his part in my healing. He chuckled at my ongoing love-hate relationship with acupuncture needles.

When he would insert the needles certain points were so sensitive and painful, sometimes I would say bad words that were preceded by the word, "Holy." He would say, "As long as you say holy first, it makes it okay."

Every time we were together we found something to belly laugh about. I adored that man. He would always be my "go-to-guy" when I needed advice about my health.

I secretly dreamed of opening a clinic with Dr. Savastio. Insurance companies aren't going to supplement the cost of alternative treatments any time soon. I wanted a place where people, who could not otherwise afford alternative treatments, could receive care at a discount or free.

Researching, understanding, and applying good nutrition and the strengthening power of vitamins, along with alternative treatments that get to the root of the problem, is how people heal and fortify physically. We could teach these principles, and I would be a great example.

Maybe some day conventional medicine will shake hands with alternative medicine and the money on the conventional side could support the researched facts of the alternative side, and the coalescing of these two just may discover a cure.

I had also seen Dr. Deschler that week. He was thrilled at my progress. I was ecstatic when he told me I had graduated to seeing him every six weeks as opposed to every three weeks. I'm indebted to both aspects of healing as they both served my different needs.

I was doing such a great job at living in the moment, but I couldn't help but dream about the day when I would only need to see him once a year. However, that would be five years from now. And I was convinced I would make it.

I knew my life was going to be magical and I would be able to help, inspire, and encourage others to love themselves to health. I could not explain how I knew this, but my knowing came from a deeply spiritual place.

That knowing carried me through the many mundane aspects of life I had to endure, like physical therapy. As a result of the surgery, I had excruciating pain in my left shoulder and could not lift it more than four to five inches.

It would take a number of months to recover. But without full motion there would be none of my beloved activities of yoga and swimming. My upper body also needed to be strong enough to ride my bike. The doctors said it could be a few years before I would be able to participate in the PMC again, but I said…"We shall see."

My dear friend, Ruthie, had registered for the 2006 PMC. Her experience of riding a bicycle was only what she remembered from her childhood, which would not support her in a 192 mile ride over the course of two, usually beastly hot days, in August.

Ruthie's reason for riding the PMC was that she had lost her partner, to breast cancer the year before I got diagnosed. She and her partner had had a dream of riding the PMC together and Ruthie promised her partner she would stay the course and do the ride. As emotional as it was, she kept her commitment to their love.

I coached her from my recliner. As weak as I still was, there was no way I could ride a bike. There was no way I could even think about riding a bike, so I lived vicariously through her. And sharing my knowledge of riding was a step toward having my own life return to normal.

Coaching her from my recliner had me excited and dreaming about the day I too would be able to, once again, mount my beautiful bicycle, Millie, and join my PMC family to peddle for a cure.

During our training visits I taught her the most effective way to ride a bike long distances. The position of her body was critical to conserve energy. I taught her she had to sit up straight but not too straight, to allow the road to pull her forward instead of trying too hard to conquer the distance. The motion of her peddling had to be fluid like that of the arm of an old fashioned railroad train; full, round, steady motion. She would need to stand up while peddling, and at first this would not be easy, but it would be a must so she could give her butt a break from the friction that could make her raw in her most tender parts.

I could not stress enough the importance of keeping herself hydrated and nourished.

That year Marsha delivered Ruthie to the starting line in Sturbridge, and I met her at the finish line in Provincetown.

***

About all I could do exercise-wise, was to turn my spare room into my own little sanctuary where I painted on a huge, six foot by four foot canvas. It was time to unleash my burgeoning creative energy, onto that oversized canvas.

By then, I had completed my year long shaman class and felt proud and acknowledged when Marc applauded me for not having missed one class despite my cancer. I had set a goal to complete the class and hadn't faltered on my commitment. During the last class we gathered in Marc's backyard and honored my feeding tube with a ceremonial burial. I felt a bit nostalgic when I buried my old friend, who just happened to have saved my life. Each person offered what it meant for them to travel alongside me over the past several months.

A ceremony seemed fitting.

During the closing ceremony Marc named me "The No Nonsense Love Goddess." I guess that said it all.

I had also said it all through the CarePages and the time had come to send my final message.

Hello dear ones,

And now the time has come to sign off the pages. It feels very bitter sweet. I will miss the connection with each of you. You have been my rock, my confidant, my angels, my keepers of the high watch, my teachers and my students. You have reached out to me with open arms and hearts that were as big as the world. The opportunity I have had to share this journey with you has completely altered my life.

It has been astounding to me to witness a community of people who came together because they genuinely cared about the welfare of someone in need. Even with your busy lives, so many of you stayed present and up-to-date with the pages. What a blessing you have been!

It would take me weeks to thank each and every one of you. So please, take this in on a personal level, and know I am holding your hands and looking you in the eyes, and saying thank you, thank you, thank you. I love you very much.

I would however like to take a moment to offer a special thank you to two very special people in my life, my sister Deleta, who, although she has a husband, six children, nine grandchildren and a very busy life, stood by my side tirelessly in support of me during this journey. No matter what, she was there every step of the way.

And my best bud Marsha, who transported me to an endless number of appointments, who would show up and would know exactly what I needed and it would be done before I even knew I needed it. Who unselfishly spent hours with me making sure I ate, and drank during those times when it was not the thing I wanted to be doing. She truly kept me alive. Thirty years is a long time for a friendship and you just can't get away with anything when someone knows you so well. Believe me I tried!

Thank you, Deleta, and Marsha, from the bottom of my heart. We had laughed hard, celebrated the best news and hung together when the news wasn't so good. You let me cry when I needed to and always held me close no matter what.

As Celine Dion sings so beautifully, "You were my strength when I was weak, you were my eyes when I couldn't see, you were my voice when I couldn't speak, you saw the best there was in me, You gave me strength 'cause you believed, I'm everything I am because you loved me". God bless you forever and ever and ever!

To each of you I say…please take very good care of yourselves, don't take anything for granted, nothing! Especially when you swallow. Take time to listen to the still small voice.

This has been the ride of my life and like I said in the beginning, "I don't have cancer, I have an opportunity." Now I have an opportunity to listen even more deeply to the still small voice and follow my bliss into the next phase of my life. My work in this world will look very different. I am ready!

Within the next few months, I will be hosting an evening at Unity on the River. It will be a wonderful time for all of us to gather. I will be speaking about what this journey has been for me and I will be sharing the power of my sound healing work.

I am looking forward to celebrating life with each of you. In the meantime, if you wish to stay connected, please send along an email and I will add you to my daily dose list.

I leave you with my favorite prayer:

> *The light of God surrounds you*
> *The love of God enfolds you*
> *The power of God protects you*
> *And the presence of God watches over you*
> *Where ever you are…God is*
> *And all is well!*
> *So be it, so it is…*
> *Namaste'*

CarePages Statistics:
Site was live: nine months
Supporters who signed on: 197
My updates: 135
Inspirational messages from supporters: 835

FIFTEEN

Smiling at My Zucchini

---

*"Accept everything about yourself--I mean everything, You are you
and that is the beginning and the end--no apologies, no regrets."-*

- Clark Moustakas

Moments after I hit the send button, to the close down CarePages, several
deeply moving messages from my loving tribe flooded in. Kelly's message
encapsulated all of them.

Auntie Denise,

*How perfect that one of your last entries on CarePages was about
jumping back into the pool at the gym. After all, you dove right in
nine months ago at that journey's start with a grace both profound
and inspired. You stretched when you needed to, pushed on when you
had to, allowed others to buoy you when the waters got rough, learned
you knew a few more strokes than you thought, and had faith that the
current would take you where you were meant to be.*

*You've inspired us all and taught us more than you'll ever know.
(For me, I've learned that I come from fierce stock and that I need
only summon my inner DeSimone girl to make it through anything!)
I'm sure others have learned equally personal lessons. But the most
amazing thing was, the drops of faith and strength and grace and love*

that your daily updates were, would ripple out from all of us who were with you on that journey and touch people you'll never know. And that's before you've written your book! I'll miss the daily touchstone that CarePages was, but I'm looking forward to the incredible feats you'll achieve on that next leg.

I couldn't be more proud to be ...your Niece Kelly.

I too was looking forward to the incredible feats I would achieve on the next leg.

Recently, I had read a most interesting article entitled, "Go Easy On Yourself – A New Wave of Research Urges."

The research suggested that giving ourselves a break and accepting our imperfections may be the first step toward better health. People who score higher on tests of self-compassion had less depression and anxiety and tended to be happier and more optimistic.

The article was talking about the immeasurable lessons I had already learned from PIN about healing myself from the inside out. The lessons learned were to stop beating myself up for nothing, to love myself unconditionally, and to make more room inside for the light of God to shine within.

The path I had been divinely guided to travel during my journey with cancer could someday potentially be a heavily traveled highway. Not only for cancer patients but for everyone afflicted with health challenges.

The fact that I was not only surviving, I was thriving, mentally, emotionally, spiritually and physically, proved the healing power of self love. Burrowing under the surface to address the origin of the problem, not just using conventional medicine to treat symptoms, was the best design for a successful healing protocol.

I knew from personal experience exercising more self-compassion, giving ourselves a break and accepting our imperfections *is* the first step toward better health. Not maybe the first step, it *is* the first and most important step.

I can imagine the day when a newly diagnosed cancer patient visits their physician for the first time. Part of their treatment protocol would include counseling sessions to teach them how to love themselves more and be more compassionate toward themselves. The protocol would arise from a new paradigm of befriending as opposed to battling cancer. Befriending the cancer would help them dialogue with it, which in turn would create more internal peace, less animosity, and would help them embrace their cancer as a teacher.

As I wove the threads from the many lessons I had learned from cancer, I would create the tapestry of my newly designed life. I wanted to interlace my personality and spirituality to create my life's purpose. I wanted to establish my purpose from a place of self-love, self-compassion and humility.

I began work with a life coach, Jackie Woodside. Jackie and I had met at Unity a few years prior to my diagnosis. In her work she combined loving and toughness, which provided a potent blend of tough love. Her assignment was to support my writing a book and to assist in the distillation and design of a clear focus on my life's purpose.

She knew how to get to the core of an issue, and how to ask provocative questions that would draw me out of my comfort zone.

During one of our telephone sessions she posed this question to me: "Did I get what I needed out of the experience I had with cancer? Good question.

I hadn't thought about what I needed to get out of it. I thought about how I would survive, and how to conjure the moxie I needed to just get through it.

As I reflected I realized I got more out of the experience than I could have ever dreamed. The major gift I received was learning to appreciate and immerse myself fully in each moment.

There were many precious moments that I had experienced. I would wake up smiling. There were days I felt like crap, had to get ready to be picked up for dreaded radiation treatments, and yet I would be smiling. Maybe it was the simple fact that I actually *woke up* that made me so happy.

The events over the past year validated my approach to journey from a place of "not having cancer," but having an "opportunity." I made the conscious decision to take a closer walk with God and not view myself as a victim. In answering Jackie's question, "Yes, I absolutely got what I needed, and a whole lot more, out of the experience."

I got the tranquility of my soul. In the way the solemnity of a quiet stream nestled deep in the mountains of Vermont, soothes the soul of an onlooker, very often I felt that kind of bliss coursing through my being.

On many occasions that deeply rooted bliss transcended recognition. It encompassed and enveloped all of me. As if everything in the universe that was good and healthy and compassionate and kind had wrapped every one of my cells in its holiness and blessed me.

While I would witness the magnificence of nature dancing with the elements, bliss saturated me with a kind of hush during quiet moments throughout the day

Just the other day, I was home alone, happily preparing dinner. Having lost almost forty pounds, and no longer dependent on my feeding tube for nutrition, I needed to gain some weight.

I had never imagined the words, "I need to gain some weight," would ever pass my lips. My heavy thighs, pocked with cellulite, were a constant source of embarrassment. I would try every exercise I could to try and shrink them. Now that I wore a size four, it really didn't matter if I was in fours or fourteens. I loved my body and I trusted its wisdom. I totally accepted myself, no matter what size I was.

The tissue in my mouth and throat was healing nicely, my esophagus was cooperating as well, and I was able to actually open my mouth wider than the width of my little finger. I had graduated from baby food to adult food.

So long as I prepared soft, overcooked foods, I was able to enjoy my culinary talents once again.

One particular evening zucchini and pasta were on the menu. While I chopped away, I smiled at the zucchini, as if we were in relationship. Smiling at my zucchini was serious business in a simple sort of way. The fact that I had been denied food for so long accentuated my appreciation of its simplicity and beauty. There were moments when I was reduced to tears by looking at the magnificence of a vegetable.

Lifting the corners of my mouth to smile at anything made me feel wonderful.

That evening the zucchini and I *were* in relationship, and I was grateful for the simple pleasures in life, while enraptured by such a natural work of art...a zucchini.

I was also deeply grateful for another of nature's unparalleled works of art, the voice. The human voice is a powerful healing instrument. For so long my voice had sounded weak, rising and falling in strength and tone.

Just eight weeks post my neck dissection, my voice was strong enough to record my "Make a Joyful Noise." CD. I was overjoyed with the quality and production. This project was the vehicle I needed in order to share with many how profound my sound healing work was.

Sound healing is an effective and proven healing modality that uses the vibration of sound to help reduce stress, and create a deep sense of peace and well being.

Sound healing helps us connect to our true rhythm by bursting through blockages that keep us trapped in the yoke of our stress. Bathing myself in the sound of my own voice, I often experienced many remarkable benefits, in particular, stress reduction.

These were some of the lessons I would share next month at Unity on the River. At my special event "Make a Joyful Noise," I had decided to incorporate my new sound healing CD as part of the program. As we join our voices in sound, we weave the fabric of our universal oneness.

Time to pray:

The oneness that I was puts my feet to my soul's purpose. Every step I take, I move in the direction of my highest and best with confidence and clarity. For this I am eternally grateful.

So be it, so it is.

In the meantime I had moved from my recliner to the gym to join Ruthie for or a few spin classes. She was gearing up for the PMC.

My strength was nowhere close to what it had been prior to my diagnosis, but I was persistent and had every confidence in my ability to regain the strength I needed to join my PMC family next year.

For now I remained focused on next steps and prepared for my special evening at Unity on the River.

Unity on The River was the perfect venue for my "Make A Joyful Noise" event because the stage was the entire length of the sanctuary, which seated over two hundred, and the professionally installed sound system filled the entire room with sound in perfect balance.

On the day of the event I arrived early to perform a sound check and make sure the place was in order, my insides shook with the reality that my dream of that evening was less than one hour away.

With everything set to go, I slipped away to meditate in Rev. Shipley's office. Hanging over the dresser in her office was a large pencil sketch of Jesus—a hippy kind of looking, Jesus.

I faced the picture and said, "Dude, with all due respect, you are my elder brother and way show-er. You helped me get here and I am counting on you to see me through. I need you beside me every moment of this evening. If I stumble and fall, stand me back up. If I cry, wipe my tears. When I speak, send angels to weave their voices with mine."

Aware of the din filtering in from the sanctuary I vibrated with excitement. I heard many elevated, exuberant voices. I guessed by the noise level, there were at least fifty people in their seats. When I heard the first notes of the pre-chosen song, as my cue to enter, I glanced back at Jesus and winked.

As John Lennon's, "Imagine" began, I walked the path from Shipley's office to center stage. In my direct line of vision was my sister Deleta. Next to her sat my brother Carlo and his daughter, Christine. Accompanying them were Kelly, her wife, Maribeth, my niece-in-law, Melanie, niece Emily, my dear friends, Marsha, Jess, Cindy, Tim, Julie, Joanie, Toni and Hank, Maryanne and Terri, and one hundred other enthusiastic people.

People sprang to their feet when they saw me walk out. They clapped loudly, cheered even louder and cried. My feet barely kissed the floor beneath me.

I headed directly for Deleta and Carlo. We smooched and exchanged a quick squeeze. I returned to center stage, stood silently, smiled while tears ran down my cheeks. I absorbed every ounce of that crowd's generous love. I imagined my arms wrapped around that exquisite master blend of humanity. I drew them close, as that moment in time cemented itself to my heart.

Once the crowd settled, I settled into the chair I had placed a few feet from the edge of the stage. The table next to me held my Biotene mouth spray that served as a temporary replacement for my deficient saliva. It also held my Tibetan Bowl for the sound healing segment, and a cup of water.

I had worried what it would be like to speak for a long period of time. I had to tell the crowd there would be interruptions during the evening when I needed to moisten my mouth—an effect of having only one remaining salivary glad. This was all part of my "new normal." This evening's venue was a safe place to practice because these people loved me.

I took a deep breath and I began with prayer:

Aboon Dabashimya (Amaraic for Great Birther)

Oh Great Birther of all that is, ever was, and will ever be, we thank you for creating us in your image. Thank you for the privilege of being alive in this now moment. You are our one true source.

As we come together this evening sharing our individual voices, we are weaving the fabric of our universal oneness. May the energy of peace and love created and shared here this evening be lifted and circulated around the great mother earth weaving a fabric for universal peace.

And may all beings be at peace.

So be it. So it is. Amen.

Sharing myself was effortless. As if they were a continuous prayer, words floated past my lips suspended in the air, and waited to be inhaled by each person.

I trusted the love that existed between each of us. It had created a safe space for me to be vulnerable and speak from my heart authentically

My survival offered each and every person the possibility and the belief, that no matter what challenge they might face, they had the power within to overcome the adversity. To be an example and an inspiration to many was why I know God chose me and held me close as I walked through to the other side.

People were intoxicated by the joy and the love that permeated the sanctuary.

The crowd enthusiastically participated in the presentation of my sound healing CD. I felt the vibration of the collective tones as they whirled about the room and shifted the energy for the benefit of each of us and the benefit of the planet.

Everything in the universe is in a constant state of vibration and therefore creates sound, including our bodies. Everything in the universe has a resonant frequency, and if our bodies are vibrating at their normal healthy frequency, we call this state health. If parts of our bodies begin to vibrate at a frequency that is not harmonious to us, we call it "dis-ease."

An important formula, I learned from Jonathan Goldman when you use sound as a healing tool is, Frequency + Intention = Healing. It was critical to bolster the sound vibration with intention. What we focus on expands, and I invited each person to set a personal intention. And I set a group intention that we wrap the energy around the planet, specifically, Palestine and Israel, to help heal the unrest that had heightened between them.

I believed the healing energy would reach its destination.

As the evening drew to a close, several people shared their personal experiences of the chakra toning. Some people were highly emotional and said the deeper we went into the tones, the more they felt their stress drip away.

They said they felt lighter, and peaceful, and happier than they had felt in a long time. I prompted them to pay attention to their desires and to honor the feelings that might surface over the next few days. I reminded them that our bodies speak to us and our emotions guide us to what we need, but most of the time we don't listen attentively. Sound healing work opens communication channels between our body, our mind, and our spirit.

I told them that loving themselves was an intention that deserved their attention. I encouraged them to honor themselves by paying close attention.

Almost everyone purchased a CD to incorporate sound healing into their personal healing repertoire. As the crowd thinned a woman I had never met approached me and bared her left forearm. "Do you know what this could be?" She pointed to the teardrops of blood that continually flowed from a single pore on her arm. I said, "No. Did something bite you?" "Nothing bit me. This happened half way through the sound healing." She looked at me and I looked at her. And we both looked down at her arm. Then she looked at me and I looked at her and I shrugged.

The next morning my stirring and stretching was interrupted by a phone call from Maryanne. She never said hello. Exuberantly, she launched into cataloging the many enchanting moments of last evening's event. Her voice quivered with excitement as she poured forth words of appreciation for what she had experienced. She said, "Denise, I am convinced, last evening's event was a portal to the future and the beginning of how you will touch and inspire many lives."

"Maryanne, I agree and I am ready, willing and almost fully able."

In two weeks it would be the one year anniversary of my diagnosis and the three month anniversary of my neck dissection. I wasn't quite as strong as I would be eventually, but each day built upon the previous and I felt stronger every day. I needed to be patient. I focused on good nutrition, meditated daily, prayed and trusted the process. Although I had no idea how my purpose in life would play out, I was excited and I trusted that when the time came I would be strong enough to answer the call.

The phone rang so quickly after disconnecting from Maryanne that I thought it was her calling back to tell me something else. So I answered by singing a long melodic, "Yeeeesssss?"

The woman at the other end asked if she could speak with Denise and I said, "This is she. I'm sorry I answered that way. I thought you were someone else. How can I help you?"

She chuckled and said, "No worries. My name is Lois and I am calling because I received a phone call this morning from a childhood friend of mine. She attended an event you had last evening someplace up North, and she had the most unusual experience while in your presence. She had what she called some type of stigmata."

Remembering the woman, I said, "Yes. She did share that with me last evening, but I'm not exactly sure what that was. And I…"

Lois interrupted me, "I've known this woman all my life. She is a pretty skeptical and conservative person. She went last night only to accompany and appease her friend. She would never tell me a story about having a stigmata appear if she didn't believe it was true." She said she was glad she went because the evening impacted her in a positive way.

"Well," I said, "I'm speechless."

Lois gets to the reason for her call, "Do you do radio interviews?"

Never having ever done a radio interview, I answered with a resounding, "Yes." Shocked at my immediate response, as the yes fell out of my mouth, I looked around the room to see who said it and had a good chuckle for myself.

Lois hosted a radio show on Monday afternoons in Brockton, Massachusetts called, "Body, Mind and Spirit." She invited me to be a guest on her three-hour call-in show.

Wow…the powers of the universe didn't waste any time drawing me through the portal of my new life. I was thrilled and humbled by how my saying yes to the work I was put here to do flooded spirit in and aligned things perfectly.

Lois and I had discussed survivorship and what had transpired for me over that past year. We set a date for the radio show and shared a heart-felt goodbye. She felt like a kindred spirit, and I looked forward to working with her.

Without removing the phone from my hand I immediately re-dialed Maryanne and shared the fantastic news.

When fabulous moments like that happen, I love how the celebrative joy jiggles and shivers us to our core.

Before I knew it, it was noontime. I had been on one call after another sharing the exciting news with friends and family. Everyone cheered and howled and slapped me an invisible high five over the phone. We all confirmed that this was the beginning of my divinely guided ministry, and we all looked forward to my maiden voyage over the radio waves.

***

Since I had discontinued the CarePages and resumed the Daily Dose, people shifted from the CarePages and signed on to receive my email messages. The recipient list had grown to over 300. The daily email was a great way to transmit information about my progress and now, my upcoming events.

The success of my sound healing CD had launched another aspect of my ministry. I had a tool accessible for others to share, and it carried my message further.

People are inspired by stories of healing, but they also want to know, "How did you do it?" and "How can I do it?"

Sound healing was just one modality I used, but it was one of the best modalities to strengthen our vibratory field which plays a big role in remaining balanced and healthy.

The evening at Unity certainly augmented my vibratory field and ushered in an excited band of angels to work with me. More requests came in for radio and television interviews.

After I was a guest on Lois's radio show, she asked if I would be interested in being a guest on her cable television show, called, "The Psychic Mind." Of course I agreed.

The most important message I shared with several cancer patients that called in was my message of self love. I suggested and requested they love themselves unconditionally and to get to the core of any unfinished, emotional business.

Maintaining good health takes a multi-pronged approach. We have to look at both what is eating us and what we are eating.

At the core of us is a bubbling warm spring of self love awaiting our arrival, inviting us to indulge in its endless supply.

Another woman who hosted a television show called "Divine Time" for cable television in Haverhill, Massachusetts approached me at church one Sunday, and asked if I would please be a guest on her show and if possible would I close with a song.

There was no better way to celebrate my upcoming birthday and the one year anniversary of my diagnosis than by sharing my story in a public way.

God rapidly answered my prayerful request to use my life in a public way to inspire others. My charge was to remain healthy and strong.

Unfortunately, staying strong meant I needed another visit to the hospital. My esophagus had shrunk and in order for me to swallow safely and comfortably I had to endure another surgical stretch.

I was extremely jittery and unsettled around this surgery because I now knew what to expect. I would not be able to eat for at least one week and it was just when I had started to get my chops down around eating a little bit.

The upside to the surgery was I would be able to enjoy some of the softer Italian treats. Six weeks to go until I would get to cash in my gift certificate that my sisters had given me for my birthday. Soon I would experience the beauty and history of Roma.

The most prudent thing anyone could do for someone looking death in the face is to give them an incentive to stay alive. While adhered to my recliner, I would almost dream myself into a trance-like state about being in Italy with my sisters. I never stopped believing I would go on the trip with them.

And the universe kept orchestrating the right and perfect situations.

Just after my birthday, my friend Cindy called to let me know room had opened up for four more people on the eight day tour that she and her family were taking to Rome. Would we (Deleta, Ed, Diane and I) like to join her and her family on the trip?

I have mentioned in other places the importance of paying attention to the messages the universe so generously sends our way. One of the things I have learned to pay attention to is when dimes show up in my life. When something is, without a doubt, in perfect alignment with the universe, dimes show up in my path as an affirmation.

The day Cindy called about the trip, I was on Cape Cod visiting Deleta. We were running an errand to CVS when my phone rang.

I was still on the call when I opened the car door to run into the store, and my eyes fell upon a bright new shiny dime. Without saying a word, I picked up the dime and flashed it at Deleta. She smiled and whispered, "There's our answer."

Each day the excitement grew stronger and stronger. I found myself nose diving into books about the sites we were going to visit. Cindy and I chatted almost daily about what clothes to pack, the expected weather in Rome, and how much room we ought to leave in our suitcase for all the leather we were going to purchase. I was giddy. I also cried tears of joy in appreciation for my life.

I was certain once we stepped foot on the soil of the old country, we would return again and again.

But first, a trip to Mass Eye and Ear.

Surgery went well. I healed quickly.

Rome – the Eternal City was exquisite! The beauty of the ancient architecture, the scooters, the food, the tastes, the smells, the music, the leather, the passion of the language, and the beauty of the people gripped my heart. I loved Italy!

As we toured the city on the first day, both Deleta and I spent the entire time wiping tears from our eyes and grinning at each other in between hugs.

When you think about Italy, you think about food. Unlike most people, I could not enjoy all of the fabulous cuisine of Rome, but I didn't allow it to diminish my joy of being there. Even the aromas wafting from café to café satisfied me. My ability to eat had been altered forever, but it had not and would never alter my desire for life.

I boarded the plane home from Italy singing, "Arrivederci Roma" and cried poignant tears, already missing it.

Sniffling back tears, I said to Deleta, "There has to be someone I know who lives in Italy. I want to return and visit the hills of Tuscany, to drink wine, and to eat pasta with the locals."

Just one week after our return, I received an email from my friend Margaret, who I had not been in contact with for over eight years. She had recently divorced and wanted to reconnect with her friends. Margaret just happened to live (are you ready?) in Paciano, Italy, a small walled village just South of where Umbria and Tuscany kiss. Her email included a plea for visitors. Fabulous! The universe was humming and responded, without delay, to my desire.

When I forwarded Margaret's email to Deleta she labeled me "a witch." A good witch of course! I'm not a witch, I just understood the power of prayer and how the laws of the universe work.

In Mark 11:24 it states very clearly, "Therefore I tell you, whatever you ask for in prayer, believe that you have received it, and it will be yours."

Through cancer I had been granted buckets of hours to ponder the power of prayer and to do the work necessary to erase out-moded patterns of behavior that were in my way of manifesting my desires. I had done the bulk of the work, and everything in me that was not in alignment with my true desires had been burned away.

I believed there would be a way for me to return to Italy because Italy fed my soul, and my desire to return was visceral. There was no reason for my desires not to be made manifest.

Within the seed of your desire is everything necessary for it to blossom to fulfillment. Another important lesson learned: The universe responds to my every request and is only interested in answering my vibration, therefore if the outcome doesn't match my desire then there is something in me that is blocking my good.

This is why it is critical to commit to practices, especially daily meditation to keep my vibration high and my channels clear.

Because the ultimate truth is…I *am* a miracle magnet.

When I am in alignment with the flow of the universe miracles flow into my life.

Plans were underway for our return trip to Italy for my next birthday, which was just ten months away.

Life Is Good!

- Sixteen -

An Unimaginable Invitation

---

*"Our deepest fear is not that we are inadequate. Our deepest
fear is that we are powerful beyond measure. It is our light, not
our darkness that most frightens us. We ask ourselves, 'Who
am I to be brilliant, gorgeous, talented, and famous?' Actually,
who are you not to be? You are a child of God. Your playing
small does not serve the world. There's nothing enlightened
about shrinking so that people won't feel insecure around
you. We were born to make manifest the glory of God that
is within us. It's not just in some of us; it's in everyone. And
when we let our own light shine, we unconsciously give other
people permission to do the same. As we are liberated from
our own fear, our presence automatically liberates others."*

- Marianne Williamson

Of all the many challenges over that year, my inability to sing topped the list. I
would cry in frustration because I could not even sing along with my guitar.

By Christmas my voice had improved but wasn't quite there yet. Now,
as I played my guitar and sang ever so softly, it moved me to tears of joy.

I had to make sure I used my knowledge of vocal toning to warm my
voice before I sang a single note. This was crucial. I wasn't able to hold notes
for too long, and some of the notes would sound squeaky, but I didn't care.
The fact that I could even eek out a note thrilled me. I was not attached
to my voice sounding exactly as it did before cancer. I was happy with

any sound. I looked forward to the day that I could sing full out. I would belt out a song with such vigor, it would overpower any deficiency. I could barely make it through a song before my mouth was too dry to continue, but I didn't care either.

Learning to sing with my newly configured neck and lack of moisture in my throat was good exercise in patience and commitment.

I was so excited to be able to submerge myself in the spirit of the holiday season. I could visit friends and family without the distraction of having to hook up to a feeding tube, or interrupt our visit because of my medication schedule.

And I was able to delight in some favorite holiday treats—mostly desserts—because they were soft and easy to manage. I had discovered a way to eat without too much distress. If I accompanied each bite of food with a small amount of liquid—not too much liquid or I would choke—and if I was careful not to swallow too quickly, I was able to eat without fear.

The doctors told me I would never eat normally again. I knew I wouldn't be able to enjoy meals the way I had over the first 50 years of my life, but that was okay. I accepted those struggles as my "new normal," and daily I found strategies to help me improve.

That December, I had excruciating pain when I ventured outdoors. Any change in temperature seemed to pressurize the left side of my neck, as if an elephant had placed its hoof against my neck. It stayed there until I went inside and warmed up. When I had to go outside, as if it were a prayer, I repeated the Buddhist saying, "All suffering comes from resisting what is." I didn't resist, I accepted all of it.

As the New Year approached, I reflected on the past year and I looked forward to what was waiting to manifest. I never make New Year's resolution. The only one I do make is to not make any. I did, however, set my intentions.

For many people resolutions are based on the idea that something is "wrong" with how they are living and needs changing. I chose to set an intention that aligned with my soul's desire and expression. My intentions felt more closely related to Divine Ideas.

These ideas would manifest through me, as opposed to my making something happen.

My intentions for that year were to see my life as blessed and to enjoy every moment of it free from worry, hurry, and anxiety.

A major intention was to move into some sort of ministry. I was uncertain how it would all manifest, but I had time to research different avenues that would offer insight into which path to follow. Shipley, the minister at Unity on the River, and I had discussed my attending Unity's ministerial school. As much as I loved Unity and its principles, I wasn't convinced that would be the right path for me. The possibility of a ministerial school that embraced all faiths appealed to me more.

I felt stronger each day. One day the 2007 Pan Mass Challenge (PMC) registration form popped into my email in-box. I found myself dreaming of doing the ride.

Rider registration had opened and spaces filled quickly, so if I was going to ride I needed to make a decision soon. Just viewing the registration form got my wheels spinning. It had been nine months since surgery and my doctors advised it would take twelve to eighteen months for a complete healing.

But I felt strong and I felt I could do it. I would commit to at least one spin class per week and by the time spring arrived I would be ready to train outdoors.

When I thought about taking to the roads I felt scared. I didn't know what it would be like riding with my disability. Would it impair my upper body strength? Would I be able to adequately turn my head to the left to keep myself safe? Could I emotionally handle it? Instead of ruminating on that much longer, I did the most productive thing I knew -- I called Marsha. "Hey, what do you think about doing the PMC with me this year?"

She said, "Count me in Mona. You know I'm your wing woman."

Next call was to Ruthie, "Hey girl, wanna ride on Denise's Dream Team for the PMC this year?

Choking back tears Ruthie said, "It would be an honor."

In the meantime, I wanted to go back to work because I needed income. As author Jim Rosemergy's book states about balancing a spiritual life and earthly living, *"Even Mystics Have to Pay the Bills."*

I contacted a prior boss who began his own start-up software company. He welcomed me onto their sales team. The job was perfect because it was part-time. Twenty hours per week. The best news was, I worked from home and the pay scale was just right.

What a gift! Part-time was all I wanted because I wanted time to travel for speaking and teaching engagements. More requests had come in to speak at Unity churches around the country, and on radio shows, but these engagements did not financially support me, yet.

I checked with Dr. Deschler to see if I could physically do the PMC. So long as my next tests came back clean, and I felt strong enough, he saw no reason why not.

The reports came back all clear. I decided it was time to register.

I wished my sister-in-law Karen's test results had been as positive as mine. Her cancer had been relentless. No matter how much chemo she absorbed and how many surgeries she endured, it would not release her from its indomitable grip.

Honestly, we needed a miracle. The thought of losing her was unimaginable and unbearable. I knew all was in divine order, but I was angry, frustrated, and reduced to fits of crying over her condition. Although I prayed for her, and affirmed her wholeness and health, from time to time I slipped into begging mode, begging God to please spare her life. Please dear God, please. Let her live.

Her family needed her. She and my brother would soon celebrate their fortieth wedding anniversary. Karen's six grandchildren adored her and she them. She had been such a warrior over these past five years. I dedicated that year's PMC to her. I knew every mile would bring us closer to a cure for Karen and so many others. I prayed she would be present to celebrate with me at the finish line, but I was terrified that was one prayer that may go unanswered.

I had to surrender to what was best for all concerned. I had to trust that God's plan for Karen, whether she lived or died was her business, not mine.

For now what I could contribute was to peddle for a cure.

With Marsha by my side, we went on line and completed our registration forms for the PMC. Along the bottom of the registration form were small boxes asking you to identify yourself. Are you a new rider? A returning rider?

Are you a survivor?

Proudly, I checked the returning rider/survivor box. The registration process alone caused my thighs to quiver. Marsha and I were so excited. We hugged, exchanged high fives and discussed a possible training schedule.

The next day I sent out a Daily Dose to announce my decision. Sharing that message with so many people created a sacred moment. My readers had witnessed me skim past death, and now I was announcing I was well enough to undertake such a feat. I was humbled. I could already hear them cheering, "You go girl."

Included in that announcement was a call for riders to join "Denise's Dream Team." A few jumped at the opportunity to ride, but most were only wishful. Most offered their financial support which I greatly appreciated.

My friend Hortensia, who was one of the first to commit to the "Dream Team," asked, "Denise, have you informed the PMC of your story?"

"No, it didn't occur to me. Do you think I ought to let them know all that has happened since the last time I rode in the PMC?"

"Absolutely, it would be a good story. I bet they would love it. Your story would be such an inspiration to others."

I sent off an email to Mary, the woman at PMC headquarters who had assisted me in setting up Denise's Dream Team webpage. I trusted she would know who to send my story to.

Good morning Mary,

I rode in '03 and then again in '05. Days after the '05 ride I was diagnosed with stage four throat and neck cancer. They gave me three months to live if I didn't move quickly and aggressively. Which I did!

I lost all ability to eat, drink water, and speak normally for a long time. For nine months, all nutrition came by way of a feeding tube in my stomach. Ten months ago I had the left side of my neck removed, muscles, nodes, etc.

This has been quite a journey, one that I would not have missed for anything.

As you know, I am doing the ride this year with nine members on the team. I am in great shape and my doctors are thrilled. I just had an MRI and all was well.

I hope my story will be an inspiration to others, give people hope, and help with fund-raising.

Any and all ideas are welcome.

Healthfully yours,
Denise DeSimone

Mary responded within minutes. She thanked me profusely for sharing my story, and congratulated me on my amazing recovery. She immediately forwarded my email to the PMC media team and was certain they would be in contact with me soon.

Twenty four hours later I received a phone call from Jill, the PMC public relations liaison. She asked if I had time for a telephone interview.

During the hour-long interview, Jill fired off numerous questions and dug deep for details as she asked questions like, "When were you diagnosed? When did you first ride the PMC? How did you handle being given three months to live? How does someone not eat for so many months?"

Over the course of the interview, she discovered I was an amateur singer, songwriter and guitarist. I told her, although the doctors warned me that my singing voice may not return, my voice was making a comeback and I was thrilled.

Jill was really excited when she learned I had recorded music that I could send along to her.

I hung up the phone and flopped, flat on my back, onto the couch, exhausted. This was the first time I had to vividly, relive the events of the past 18 months. I had a headache from scraping the inside of my brain, pulling out the information needed to answer her many probing questions. Hard as her questions were, I knew they were inspired by genuine concern and curiosity.

As I listened to myself tell my own story, I felt so much stronger than the person I was describing. It was as if I had been speaking about someone else. *Who was that woman who went through hell to stay alive?*

The remainder of that day I dedicated to training. It was April, and I was going to ride Millie for the first time since August 2005.

Marsha and I headed to the industrial park, where I would not be distracted by any traffic. We were excited, eager, nervous and apprehensive. I was astounded by how nervous I was. In the past I had been such a brassy but always cautious cyclist who rode with confidence and fearlessness.

Today...not so much.

Marsha loaded my bike on the rack and checked all my gear. Then we headed for the industrial park.

Marsha took Millie off the rack and positioned her in front of me and just smiled. As I swung my leg over and mounted Millie, the butterflies in my stomach fluttered throughout my entire core. I was so happy to be reunited with my ride. Her light blue frame was all shiny and bright. I wore my light blue bike shirt so Millie and I would match.

Marsha and I spun around the safe, quiet streets of the industrial park a few times and I began to feel a little daring. It didn't take long for me to regain my confidence, so I spun up next to Marsha and said, "Okay Marshie, I'm ready. Let's head down Scotland Rd."

We turned out of the park, headed west and never looked back.

Our morning trainings were so special because I loved being out doors so early in the day. I loved the feel of the wind as it brushed against my skin. And how the clean fresh air felt as it filled my lungs. Most days we surpassed our goal of twenty miles.

PMC day was the first Saturday in August, and it was most always a sizzling hot day, so Marsha and I had to be in the best possible shape.

I felt strong and knew I would get even stronger over the next few months. Marsha couldn't believe how I had regained my "road warrior, biker chick" status so quickly.

My newfound strength came from a deep emotional place. It was Karen's imminent demise that would drive me to exertion. I thought, if I rode faster, harder, stronger, longer, somehow, in some crazy way, this would help her pull through.

I knew this made no sense but neither did her dying. The juxtaposition of my strength and her weakness boggled my mind and crushed my heart.

When I visited her, always lovingly surrounded by my brother and their children, I actually felt guilty that I was doing so well and she, after fighting so hard for so long, was nearing the end of her short sixty one years.

Again, this made absolutely no sense but these feelings were real and I had to acknowledge them. I wasn't quite sure how to process all of it, but riding helped me.

All these feelings helped to fuel my trainings. There were times I thought about Karen and I would sob and push on through the tears. The more I cried the harder I pumped my legs and the faster I went, until I was exhausted. Afterwards, feeling physically and emotionally spent somehow made me feel better.

Most often I was in the lead so Marsha was unaware of my tears. To her I was just doing what Mona did: taking the lead.

I was so busy with work, training and scheduling upcoming speaking engagements, I had forgotten about the interview with the PMC media folks.

Until one day, toward the end of May, I received a phone call from Jill.

"We want to run your story in your local paper, The Daily News in Newburyport, and we need your permission. Do we have it?"

Squealing inside, but with a soft calm voice, I responded, "Sure that would be great." So many people had been inspired by my story, and this would be a terrific way to spread the message even further. It would also help boost our fund-raising efforts. The story she had written was a perfect documentation of the facts, so I blessed it and they sent it off to the presses at the Daily News in Newburyport.

A few weeks later, the front page story was my story: "CANCER SURVIVOR RIDES FOR A CURE." My photo was front and center. The article was a catalyst in support of the fund-raising efforts of "Denise's Dream Team" And more importantly, the Jimmy Fund kids.

But the cure didn't come soon enough for Karen. I could not remember a time when such sadness had permeated my entire family.

She and Johnny did celebrate their 40th anniversary. She also hung on long enough to see her little grandchild Grace, who was born just a few days before her death, on the 5th floor, just below Karen, at the same hospital.

Her final resting place was a quaint little cemetery on Cape Cod nearby their home in Pocasset. My brother John continued to spend each day visiting with his beloved Karen. And I kept riding. I would picture her sweet face at the top of each grueling hill, encouraging me to conquer them one at a time. I thought of her often, and would think of her each year on September 10th. We shared the same birthday.

Life was pretty quiet during those days. I conserved my energy for training and work. I took long walks and communed with nature. As I walked I invoked prayers of thanks for my continued improved health.

I was also able to bump up my appointments with Dr. Deschler to every three months as opposed to every six weeks. This was such a relief because every examination involved the insertion of a scope with a camera at the end of it. It traveled up my nose and down my throat checking for any growths. Then he always apologized before he had to gag me by sticking his index finger down my throat. Then he would swipe his finger across the deepest point of the back of my tongue to make extra sure he couldn't feel anything out of the ordinary.

He would glow after each time he examined me. "All good," he would say.

I sensed he was proud of me for taking such good care of myself and for stepping up to do the ride again. I couldn't imagine he had many patients like me. It must be tremendously gratifying for a doctor to witness a patient thrive after being so close to death.

I was proud of him too, and the fine artistry he performed on my neck. The scar on my neck was finally softening, it no longer looked like the face of a Shar Pei dog, all gathered up and folded together. He told me it was necessary for him to stitch the incision in that way so as time passed the scar would soften and my neck would look as normal as possible.

Each time I checked the PMC donations page, the thermometer was inching its way daily toward our goal. My personal fund-raising goal that year was $8,000 and the team goal, $25,000. With the type of print exposure my story had been receiving, I knew we would reach or maybe even exceed our goals.

I inspired the Dream Team with emails daily. I praised them for their effort and commitment and let them know how much I appreciated and loved them for taking a stand against the epidemic of cancer. We tried to organize group rides but it was a challenge. Hortensia, Joanie, and Lissette lived so far away that it was easier for them to train independently. Stephanie, Marsha, Peter, Ruthie and I had ridden together a few times, which was a preview to what it would be like riding together on our special day.

One morning after sending out a team email, I unassumingly clicked on an email from a woman named Meredith at PMC Headquarters.

Dear Denise,

First, I just want to say that I read a bit about your story (Jackie, Jill's manager, at Teak Media told me about you) and you are an amazing woman!!

Secondly, I am writing to ask you if you would honor us by singing the National Anthem at the Wellesley Start on Saturday August 4th on PMC weekend. I believe that you are registered to start from Babson so I was hoping that you would be available to sing at our ceremonies at 7:30 and then start with the rest of the group on your ride to Bourne.

We can discuss details and I will look forward to meeting you in person but I just wanted to invite you with enough notice to make some plans. I hope you will consider being part of our opening ceremonies and hope to hear from you soon.

Take care, Meredith

Once again my heart pounded out a clarion thump…thump…thump, the way it pounded in the doctor's office at Mass Eye and Ear so many months ago. Now, the reason for the pounding was far more gratifying.

I wanted to make absolutely sure I read this email correctly, so I re-read it, and read it again. As I reached for my telephone to call Deleta, I realized I had left it in the other room. I motioned in that direction but I felt like somehow glue had been applied to my butt. I was stuck. I felt like I could have jumped out of my skin but I couldn't move. I would say that's the paradox of pure, raw excitement.

A barrage of questions flooded my mind. Can I do it? The National Anthem is such a tough song to sing, can I even sing it? Even if I could, would I be able to sing it in front of four thouuuuuusand PMC people? What if I freak out? What if my voice isn't strong enough? Should I just say yes and figure it all out later?

My head buzzed like a swarm of bees had invaded my brain.

Twitching with excitement, I conference called Marsha and Deleta and read them Meredith's email. It was clear to them I was excited, but I was also scared that I would not be able to sing. I needed them to help me decide whether or not to say yes.

Deleta reminded me what an honor and a privilege it was to sing the National Anthem, she also said, "Not only that, I believe you can do it, your voice is stronger by the day, honey. What an amazing venue to share your new-found voice. What an inspiration you would be to others. How could you not accept the honor?"

Everything Deleta said was logical. How could I not accept the invitation? This was an honor, a privilege and a phenomenal venue for inspiration.

I composed myself while I composed the email to Meredith to let her know I was honored and I would be happy to sing the morning of the ride.

Meredith was elated by my acceptance. During a conversation the following week, she nonchalantly said that I would share the stage that morning with Larry Lucchino, the President and CEO of the Boston Red Sox, and Ed Benz, the President of The Dana Farber Cancer Institute in Boston.

The Boston Red Sox are the presenting sponsor of the PMC and are very involved in all PMC events. I have been a devoted Red Sox fan from the time I was in the womb. Not only would I be sharing the stage with the President and CEO of the Boston Red Sox organization, but I had to sing the National Anthem while he was standing next to me?

Alrighty then...

Here's a bit of history. I have been a dedicated Red Sox fan from the time I was a child. My two older brothers desperately wanted a little brother. I think I was eight or nine years old before they realized I was a girl. My mother thought I was born with a baseball glove on my left hand. When I wasn't playing catch with my brother or the neighborhood boys, I occupied myself for hours with a tennis ball. I bounced it off the wall across the street, using the gate stop in my neighbor's driveway as my pitchers mound. I would play a full nine innings. I was happy to a part of the PMC but I was equally excited to be in the presence of Larry Lucchino.

As thrilling as all this was, my job was to take good care of myself on all levels. I had to make sure I was getting enough calories each day while training for the ride.

I also needed to spend some time planning the next phase of my life. I researched many different options for ministerial school and had decided that beginning in September, I would attend classes at ChIME, The Chaplaincy Institute of Maine.

They were an interfaith wisdom school and open community committed to transformation of the self and planet earth through education, ordination, support, celebration and service. It was a perfect match for what I wanted in a ministerial school.

I was so excited about embarking on this new phase of my personal and professional life. ChIME's satellite office in Massachusetts made it convenient for me to attend their two year program. This program aligned with my desire to create a ministry that encompassed all faiths.

Just about the time I didn't think life could get more exciting, the universe whipped up an unimaginable invitation.

One early morning in late June my phone rang. The woman introduced herself as Jackie from Teak Media.

After we exchanged a few pleasantries, she told me the reason for the call. "I want to discuss something with you. How would you like to sing the National Anthem at Fenway Park before the Red Sox game on July 14th ? It's PMC night at Fenway. There will be thousands of riders in the stands, as well as one hundred plus survivors on their bicycles surrounding home plate supporting you while you sing." Jackie adds, "So what do you think? Will you do it?"

"How did all this come to pass?"

Jackie explained, "Billy Starr, the PMC's founder and Executive Director, and his wife Meredith were notably moved by your story and how you had embraced your cancer as opposed to battling it. They are incorporating your message into this year's PMC message. They ran your story by the decision makers at Red Sox headquarters, and they all decided it's you they want to sing the National Anthem at our special evening."

This all happened much faster than I had envisioned.

I had put myself out there requesting that the universe support my desire to play big, and now it had snowballed into an energy I wasn't sure I could handle.

Singing at Babson College the morning of the ride was a huge honor but paled in comparison to now singing to a Fenway Park audience.

Once able to speak, I strung a few words together and responded to Jackie.

"I am truly humbled by their invitation. This is such an honor. I wish I could say yes in this moment but I cannot. If it is all the same to you, I would like a day to meditate on this to see if this is mine to do."

With a gentle and soft voice Jackie said, "I can't wait to meet you. Take all the time you need. Here's my cell phone number. Call me when you have made your decision."

My hands vibrated as I dialed Deleta's number. "Dee, it's me. Do you have a minute?"

"Not really. Diane is out in the car waiting for me to go shopping. Can I call you later?"

"No. I need to speak to both of you right now. Please call me when you get in the car and put me on speaker phone."

Concerned Deleta asked, "Is everything okay?"

"Yes, I'm fine. Talk to you in a minute."

I answered in a nanosecond. "Am I on speaker phone?"

Diane answered the question with, "Yes honey, we're here. What's going on? Are you okay?"

Choking back tears I said, "I'm fine. I have to tell you what just happened." As I wiped tears from my cheeks with my bare hands, I shared the latest news.

None of us believed it. We had been side by side on my journey for nearly eighteen months. We were still so sad, mourning the loss of our Karen.

Although the exquisite joy and the tenderness of our suffering were separated by only millimeters, the excitement of that moment was uncontainable.

Once we calmed ourselves, Diane's first statement put it all into perspective.

"Honey, this is what you asked for. Remember? Imagine how much of an inspiration you will be to so many people that evening? How can you not do it?"

Diane was absolutely correct. I did ask for my life to be used as an inspiration to many. My decision was made. I only needed to know "why" and leave the "how" for God to figure out and this was obviously God's answer to "how." I would not interrupt the flow of this magical energy by saying no.

"I love you both so much." I hung up the phone and retreated to my meditation chair.

I sat for almost two hours. As I recapped the past eighteen months of my life, it all whirled around inside me: the ride in 2005, the diagnosis, the painstaking doctor's appointments, the surgeries, the radiation, the debilitating side effects of so many treatments and infections, the crazy chemo day, the entire cast of amazing people who stood by me for all those months, and the continuous conversation with God about using my life for a higher purpose.

This news would spread through my tribe with an incomprehensible excitement. I couldn't wait for their reactions.

I would be covered with goose bumps whenever I thought about stepping onto that storied field and standing at home plate where so many greats had celebrated so many historical moments. That would be as much an honor as singing the National Anthem.

I didn't share the news with Marsha over the phone. I asked her to come by when she had a chance. She sensed the importance of my request and arrived almost immediately. We hugged so tightly and cried so hard and laughed so loudly, all at the same time.

My family, my friends and I had sailed on the friendship ship for almost two years. They stood at the helm, the stern, the bow and the wheel. And I charted the course.

I was thrilled by the level of merriment the news of my debut at Fenway had brought to so many lives. We relished and reveled in the magnificence of the moment.

I would be the one who gets to walk on the field representing the force and fierceness of the love that people hold for one another during tough times. This was not just about me. It was about each of us. It was a powerful and shining example of how together we could conquer anything.

Just as a kid awaits Santa on Christmas Eve, I waited for PMC night at Fenway Park, home of the Boston Red Sox.

- SEVENTEEN -

Oh Say Can You Sing

"...o'er the land of the free, and the home of the brave."

- The United States National Anthem

The first week of July, with only ten days to go, Jackie from Teak Media had forwarded promotional information to every local newspaper. Several of the reporters had been in contact with me to schedule interviews and photo shoots.

My sister Diane had jumped into the media frenzy as well. She contacted The News Tribune, the local newspaper in our hometown of Newton. They too wanted an interview and would run the story a few days before the event at Fenway.

I just wanted to rest my voice and practice singing the National Anthem, but all the coverage served a greater purpose of raising awareness and funds, so I needed to rally.

The interviews were much less arduous than the initial one with Jill from Teak Media. It wasn't as painful having to excavate the details. Each reporter asked about my endurance and how I had managed to arrive at a place of such strength and conviction.

The reporters were all well spoken and sensitive, and I was certain they would do my story justice.

In the meantime, I kept riding my bike and practiced my song while I eagerly awaited the newspaper delivery boy.

When they arrived the newspaper articles were so well-written. The photographs had perfect placement, and each reporter captured the highlights of my story and delivered my message with eloquence.

All the excitement was also mixed with moments of sadness and deep humility.

Strangers approached me in public places and thanked me for being such an inspiration. They shared stories of their personal struggles with cancer as well as stories of loved ones who had passed on from cancer. Perfect strangers would hug me passionately while they murmured heart-felt thank yous.

It was a gift to be honored as a survivor and recognized as someone who had a higher purpose. This was my second chance at life, and I would press on and continue to search for places where I could support and inspire others.

The schedule for the singer who would be singing the national anthem at Fenway Park included a rehearsal on the Friday afternoon, prior to the weekend games.

That Friday, Marsha and I headed to the rehearsal. My cell phone rang and Jackie from Teak Media says, "Denise, would you mind if a few news reporters from nationally syndicated television shows meet you at Fenway Park to interview you?"

I repeated the question aloud so Marsha could hear what she just asked. I accompanied my words with a sideways glance and a smirk and raised my eyebrows as a silent substitute for my asking, "What should I do?" Of course I already knew the answer.

Her face radiated with an unmistakable, "YES."

"Yes of course, Jackie. That would be great. I wish I had known I would be appearing on the evening news, I would have been more particular about my attire." Jackie assured that whatever I was wearing would be fine and said,

"Call me on your way home to let me know how it went."

When Marsha and I arrived at the park, the reporters and camera crews were waiting just outside the gate. Media people are not allowed into the park unless they are accompanied by the interviewee. Together we entered the park and headed for home plate. I stepped onto the field and the crew immediately hooked a tiny microphone to my shirt and hooked a small pack onto the back of my pants.

It was awe-inspiring as I stood ON THE FIELD at home plate in historic Fenway Park. The park was empty. So still and silent. The rich, green, cushiony grass felt as if I was standing on the most expensive carpeting in the entire world. Even the dirt looked clean. How was it possible that even dirt could look clean? It was because everything about that day was magical.

I envisioned millions of fans whose voices lingered in the rafters. Over the years groans of disappointment as well as cheers of euphoria had filled this park. Millions of fans throughout the years had mourned losses year after year of the team who would come so close to winning the World Series.

Finally the curse had been broken when we captured the title in 2004 and ended our eighty-six-year drought. The history was all there, hovering, and I drank it in like a thick, tall, icy cold protein drink.

I did my best to remain focused on the conversation Dan, the sound person for Fenway, and I were having about the position of the microphone. He asked, "Do you want a hand-held mic or a stationary mic?"

"Stationary sounds good and safe." I said.

As I stepped to the mic, I closed my eyes for a brief moment, took a deep breath and sang the entire National Anthem to an invisible crowd of 35,000 Red Sox fans.

The rehearsal ended and I sat with the first of two local reporters. She was a delightful woman with a bright, kind face. She asked all the appropriate questions about my journey, in particular what it was like to lose my voice and have it return as strongly as she just witnessed. The entire interview took about fifteen minutes. Once that interview ended, I had to move to another section so the background would be different for the reporter from the competing station.

The footage from both interviews would appear on the six o'clock news, and I couldn't wait.

On the way home Marsha and I slapped some high fives, smiled a lot and phoned everyone to tell them to turn on the evening news.

Marsha sat on the couch. I was too excited to sit so I stood in the middle of my living room, eight inches from the television screen, and we waited for the six o'clock news. We were so excited we couldn't even speak.

There it was, my "pinch me" story on major networks, complete with headshots plastered all over the screen, along with me riding Millie. The anchor people appeared to be visibly moved as they told my story with such deep regard for my journey. I expected the segment to be about one minute, but it turned out to be close to three.

The reporters had done a fantastic job.

My emotions were collected and knotted at the base of my throat. Although I reveled in the extraordinary, outrageous, excitement of the event, I needed to relax and get a good night's sleep. This was imperative in order to be prepared for tomorrow.

Marsha gave me a big strong hug and said, "Great job Mona. Get some rest my friend. I love you. See you tomorrow."

I loved that some of the news footage had included Marsha. It felt appropriate to see us both on television. After all…we're a team!

The day had arrived in absolute beauty, with crisp cool air and not a cloud in the sky. The weather report for that evening called for the same.

Clear skies and cool temps. Perfect!

It was a pensive kind of day as I quietly contemplated the evening. The only person I saw that day was Ruthie. Ruthie's profession was a massage therapist. She had come over to give me a relaxing foot rub.

She knew I didn't want to use my voice much, so every now and then we would lock eyes and grin silently.

During our session my cell phone rang but I chose not to interrupt my massage. Once the session ended I listened to the message. It was a woman, Linda, whom I had never met. I first listened to the message privately; then I pushed the speaker phone button, hit the replay button and drew Ruthie into listening.

This woman's message was full of pain and sadness. She had been given my name and number from someone at the Cancer Center at the Concord Hospital in New Hampshire.

On the message she explained she was a throat and neck cancer survivor and that over the past few months she had had a recurrence. She had two young girls whom she adored and could not imagine leaving them alone. Through her tears, she asked if I would please return the call to offer some words of inspiration and to share any ideas I might have about alternative therapies.

I pressed the "end" button. Ruthie and I continued to stare into each other's eyes just as we had been doing while we listened to the entire message.

Tears welled up in my eyes. I bowed my head and shook it from side to side, in disbelief of what I had just heard.

I needed an hour after Ruthie left to prepare for the call to Linda.

"Hello Linda, my name is Denise DeSimone."

Her wounded heart traveled across the wire as she said, "Thank you so much for returning my call."

The conversation was tender. For a person who has had throat cancer, a recurrence is frightening because radiation is no longer an option. There is only a certain amount of radiation that a body can absorb.

Linda's doctors were hopeful, but treatment would now mean debilitating chemotherapy. She and I discussed the many options available and I suggested she visit my website where she could learn more about the alternatives I found to be the most beneficial.

I told her I was a chaplain and I asked, "Linda, would you be interested in praying with me?" Before we prayed I asked, "Do you beg God when you pray, which is totally understandable if you do, or do you pray in a way that affirms your wellness, wholeness and strength?"

Before she answered the question, I gave her an example of the type of prayer I was referring to.

Excitedly she interrupted me, "Yes, yes, that's how I want to learn to pray. I don't pray that way but that's how I want to pray." I comforted by telling her we would end our conversation in prayer.

"Linda, why did you choose to call me? Did you see me on television or read about my story in any newspaper?"

The pitch of her voice escalated which indicated her curiosity, "No. Why would I have seen you on television or read about you in the newspaper?"

I shared what I was about to do in a few hours and she exclaimed, "I cannot believe you're singing the National Anthem at Fenway Park in a few hours and you have just spent all this time consoling me. I'm so sorry. If I had known I never would've called you today. I've had this card with your number on it for over a month. I have no idea why I chose today to call you."

I kept my voice calm to balance out her heightened energy, "I know why you chose to call me today. Today's the ideal day for you to call me. As monumental and as exciting as singing the National Anthem at Fenway Park will be, you are the reason I am making my journey public. Your journey with cancer, your surviving cancer, your wanting to stay alive for your children, your reaching out to me with the possibility that together we can co-create something, anything, whatever it might be for you to feel better. That's what this night is all about. God has a way of keeping us all humble, Linda, and I could not be more grateful for the lesson in humility at this moment. You're an angel in my life. Thank you for coming into my life today."

Before we prayed I told Linda, "While I'm singing the National Anthem tonight, I'll be singing it particularly for you."

We cried our way into prayer.

There was absolutely no doubt that I was but a messenger placed here to serve. If even for one moment I began to operate from the slightest egotistical place about being chosen for such an honor, spirit had just reminded me about the power of modesty and what my true purpose was.

My dearest friend Douglas had offered to drive me to Fenway Park. He was the perfect gentleman and the absolute perfect chauffeur because of his pleasant and calm demeanor. He tolerated my vocal exercises in the car on the way in as I warmed my voice and practiced a few bars of the song.

When we arrived at Fenway the place was swarming with PMC riders, bicycles, people in their bike garb, media. PMC night was a big deal. I knew there were thirty friends and family members peppered throughout that amazing park ready to support me.

I stepped onto the field with most of the thirty standing behind home plate peeking through the mesh fence that separated home plate from the fans.

I didn't know my brother Johnny was going to be there until I heard his all familiar whistle. He's one of those guys who can whistle through his teeth, never putting his hand to his mouth, yet delivering an ear piercing whistle that grabs your attention.

I heard the whistle and my head spun in that direction. I saw him ascending the stairs next to home plate. He didn't quite come all the way down to greet me. From a few feet away he nodded. And with a bent elbow, he pumped his clenched fist in the air. I knew exactly what he was saying, "Go get'm kid."

I was happy he didn't come all the way down to greet me. If I had hugged him it might have caused a meltdown and I could not cry at that moment. I had to harness every bit of that emotion to sing for Karen and Linda, and others un-named who deserved to be free from the ravages of cancer.

A few moments later the boisterous voice of the Fenway announcer reverberated through the park, "Ladies and gentlemen, tonight's National Anthem is being sung by a two time PMC rider and throat cancer survivor, Denise DeSimone."

During his introduction, one hundred Pan Mass Challenge survivors entered from behind the Green Monster (the center-field wall). They biked along the warning track and arrived at home plate and encircled me. They lined up along the first base line and third-base line like warriors. I felt as if each and every one of them had wrapped their arms around me in support of my journey and their personal history.

With my Biotene in hand, I pressed for one final squirt, and stepped up to the mic. The cacophony of the crowd had been silenced by the announcer's voice.

I looked straight ahead and tilted my head back slightly, and chose to focus on the number 26 which identified the section directly in front of me.

I took a deep breath and began to sing, "Oh say can you see by the dawn's early light what so proudly we hail at the twilights last gleaming."

I was totally engrossed as I sang for Linda and Karen. By the time I got to, "Oh say does that Star-Spangled Banner yet wave," the entire crowd had begun to sing along. The minute I ended the thunderous applause rippled through the stands directly into my heart. I felt my heart open to match the expansiveness of that glorious park. I inhaled that moment and saturated my soul with the support of the crowd, and I silently thanked God for my life, especially for my resilient voice.

"Play ball," were the next words we all heard. Within moments David Ortiz whacked one out of the park. Again the crowd roared and I knew it would be a great game.

Immediately after I sang, the station that sponsored the event whisked me off for an interview that lasted approximately fifteen minutes.

After the interview, the reporter said to her camera man, "She's a media darling. Follow her as she makes her way to her seat. This will be great footage for tonight's segment."

We headed to our seats, which were perched up high in the grandstands. With the camera man in tow filming my trek, I began my approach; thousands of fans stood and began to applaud. The higher I climbed, section by section, more fans began to stand as the news spread, "Here comes the woman who sang the National Anthem."

It felt as if hundreds of people tried to reach out to me to hug me and high-five me. I heard a few people say, "God bless you" as I passed by them. It was like a mini wave.

When I finally reached my designated seat, my sister Deleta was crying. She said, "What a momentous event! I missed most of it because I was crying so hard I could not see. You were amazing. Watching you making your way to your seat was the most exciting moment for me. When I saw the crowd all around us standing and cheering, and looking to the right, I could see the people in the stands beside us on the right looking to the left and cheering. I couldn't see so I asked Eddie, 'What's happening, why is everyone cheering?' He smiled at me and said, 'It's for your sister. She's trying to get to her seat."

Deleta and I hugged and she handed me my dinner, an icy cold, protein drink that I had prepared earlier. That protein drink tasted like sweet nectar from heaven.

I exhausted quickly and had to leave the game early. People recognized me as I exited the park and once again, I was congratulated, high fived, hugged and was offered words of gratitude and praise.

This was another one of those ineffable moments in my life.

I was the most fortunate person on the planet. It's an understatement to say that it was an honor and a privilege. I could only imagine the percentage was sky high of how many people in the stands were suffering from cancer at that moment or who among was mourning the loss of a loved one to cancer. For each of those beautiful, special souls it was humbling to be in their presence and sing for them.

When I returned home my email in-box was overflowing with emails from family, friends, and total strangers. One of the more poignant was this email from a fellow cancer survivor.

Denise,

I was at Pam Mass Challenge Night at Fenway Park. It was a big night for my family and I since it was my kids' first ball game. It was such a wonderful event. The biggest moment that impacted us the most was your performance of the National Anthem. After seeing you sing I had to email you how much my family and I were moved. I am a two time cancer survivor so being at that event was wonderful in itself. Your performance was very powerful and I don't think there was one dry eye in the entire stadium. Your performance was a great reminder of what being a survivor is all about. Sometimes we forget about that great second chance in life. Thank you for reminding me. I was so glad to be here (alive) to have seen your performance.

Your fellow cancer survivor

Steven

This message epitomized how important it is for us to take back our lives. And how important it is to grow even stronger after being mowed down by cancer.

The emails were powerful. The head radiation technician at North Shore Cancer Center where I had received my treatment was at the game. She had been unaware that she was about to witness me sing. In her email she said, "It was one of my proudest moments."

An oncologist from Seattle sat in the row behind Hank and Toni. When he found out they were friends of mine he asked for my contact information. He sent me an e-mail thanking me for demonstrating incredible strength, courage and faith.

He also said my ability to sing had brought tears to his eyes because no one there realized better than he that treatment for head and neck cancer is the most difficult cancer treatment there is. And that my singing the way I did was a miracle.

I could attest it had been the most difficult treatment, and I believed each and every treatment was difficult. It doesn't matter what type of cancer diagnosis someone is handed, each person's personal journey is the most difficult, and that is why we have to come together, take a stand and find a cure.

This was why each of us made the commitment to ride while we held the PMC motto deep within our hearts: "Closer by the Mile."

A few days after I sang at Fenway I was contacted by The New England Council. This organization was comprised of presidents of all major corporations and top seeded politicians from all across New England.

They invited me to sing the National Anthem at their annual dinner in October in at a very swanky hotel in Boston. My brother-in-law, Ed laughed and said, "Looks like you have a new career as a professional National Anthem singer."

It was an honor to be invited to sing at their meeting, and I graciously accepted but my focus was on being in the best possible shape for the upcoming ride.

EIGHTEEN

Ride Millie Ride.

"Closer by the mile."

- The PMC motto

Over those next few weeks I had to make sure I was prepared physically, mentally and emotionally to ride 87 miles in one day.

Although I had already sung the National Anthem at Fenway, singing for my peer riders and survivors at the opening ceremony the morning of the ride would be a more intimate experience for me. There was absolutely nothing that compared to the unity felt among the riders on Pan Mass Challenge day.

It's like we are all one mind, one heart, and share one single purpose: to find a cure. I felt strong. I felt ready. I was excited and humbled.

It was the eve of the ride and several of my friends and family had committed to meet me at the opening ceremonies early the next morning.

Marsha came over that evening and we watched the "PMC Kick Off" on NECN, televised from Sturbridge. That was where the starting line was for the two day riders.

Billy Starr hosted the show and interviewed the most amazing people, some of whom had ridden each year for the past several decades. The hour long tribute was rich with touching stories of personal triumph and determination. Tears flowed as we watched the presentation.

Meredith had extended an invitation for me to join them that evening, but I had to decline. I wanted to be well rested and in good voice for the morning.

The show was a real tribute to all of us. This year I felt even closer to each of the riders and hoped I had made a difference in each of their lives by my demonstration of strength and determination.

Marsha and I sat side-by-side on the couch gearing up to ride side-by-side in the morning.

As I stirred early the next morning, I thoroughly enjoyed the foggy moments it took to call forth the day's events. As the mental images of the day played out before my eyes, I powered myself out of bed, jumped into the shower and put on my dragonfly bike shirt.

Tim and my sweet friend Brooks had offered to be our "Road Angels" this year. They would arrive soon to caravan it to Babson College.

It was a bit too early to practice the national anthem in my condo complex, so I hummed quietly to warm my voice. I knew I would have plenty of time on the drive in to entertain the troops.

Before I left the house, I taped a 5 x 7 photo of Karen and me to the utility bag that was attached to my handle bars. The photo had been taken at last year's Relay for Life. I knew the ride would be easier with her to watch over me.

Our bags were packed and the team arrived. The bikes were loaded and we began the first leg of the day's trek.

When we pulled onto the campus at Babson, I was astounded to see how many family members and friends had honored their commitment to meet me at the opening ceremonies.

Meredith was so happy to see me. She hugged me tightly and escorted me over to the dignitaries who stood beside the stage. She proudly introduced me to Larry Lucchino, The President and CEO of the Red Sox Organization and Ed Benz, President and CEO of The Dana Farber Foundation. They seemed genuinely pleased to meet me, and I was overjoyed at meeting them.

I'm not usually a star-struck kind of girl, but I did get a bit giddy as I stood next to the "guy who gets it all done" at Red Sox headquarters.

Meredith introduced me to the crowd as the "woman who sang the National Anthem" at PMC night at Fenway, and the crowd erupted with applause.

Then, I stepped to the podium, adjusted the microphone and gazed out over the massive, silent sea of bikers. I began to sing. I cast my eyes over the colorful crowd and stared straight ahead, to the opposite end of the parking lot, where "Old Glory" waved majestically in the wind.

The moment I finished singing, Larry grabbed my shoulders and hugged me. He left his hands stuck to my shoulders, looked directly into my eyes, paused and said, "Throat cancer my ass." After another forceful hug from him, a hug from Ed and one from Meredith, I jumped off the stage and I headed for Millie.

We took the final team photos, exchanged our final hugs and I offered the Prayer of Protection for each of us, the riders and all volunteers. We firmed our plans to meet at a designated spot at the lunch stop. The "Road Angels" Tim and Brooks, would arrive before us to set up lunch so there would be no delay in getting us back on the road.

The starting gun was fired and the riders filed underneath the towering arch of multi-colored balloons. Once again, hundreds of riders began the ride bike dancing to the powerful voice of Bono as we all wheeled off to the tune, "It's a Beautiful Day."

It certainly was a beautiful day. I could not have been more proud of "Denise's Dream Team." They trained rigorously and had raised over $25,000 and we had several more months to continue our fundraising effort.

Crowds lined the streets with posters covered with photos of loved ones who had been afflicted with cancer. Far too many posters carried the sad words, "In memory of."

We spun our way into the second water stop where I noticed my nephew Greg, his wife Colleen, and their daughter Cecilia. Their heads bobbed back and forth through the flow of riders as they tried to identify us in the crowd. Greg was Karen's son and my godchild. We didn't exchange too many words. They wanted to know how I was doing and if I needed anything. I told them I was doing great and I thanked them for being there to support us. We hugged a few times and the girls and I headed for the water bottles.

More than ever, as I looked into my nephew's eyes, I wished there had been a cure.

Marsha, Lissette and I maintained a steady pace of thirteen to fourteen miles per hour. At that pace we would surely roll into the lunch stop at our predicted time.

Throughout the day riders had recognized me by the name tag that hung from the back of my seat. They would cruise up beside me and thank me for the great job I did singing the national anthem that morning. Several of them mentioned they had heard me sing at Fenway and how proud they were of me.

A few of the short conversations I had were teary, as people shared with me their motivation for doing the PMC. If we had not been rolling down the road on our bikes. we would have hugged, so we settled for a quick hand embrace. I was honored to be a part of this tenacious and dedicated PMC family.

Brooks and Tim were so excited as they watched us roll into the lunch stop. They had spread a blanket underneath a shady tree and emptied the contents of the cooler onto the blanket. We had quick and easy access to all the goodies. I was starved!

One by one the Dream Team arrived. It was good fun to listen to the stories of how they tackled this hill and that hill. The people they had met along the way, and the posters and people that had caught their attention.

I fell more in love with these people every time I was in their presence. I felt like the proud parent. Although we all wished we could cross the finish line together, we each rode at different speeds and understood it would not be possible. We made a pact to wait for each other at the end of the ride in Bourne.

It was only forty miles to the finish line! There were some ambitious hills on the last leg. The temperature had risen and so had my feelings of joy. Thinking about the after party fueled me to conquer the remaining monstrous hills.

Deleta and Ed had prepared a delicious Italian spread for all of us to enjoy back at their home. and I could not wait to take a hot shower, slip into my skinny jeans and eat some fattening food.

The next twenty miles were grueling. The 90 degree temperature wore on us and the full sun beat us up. The hills seemed steeper than I had remembered. I pictured Karen's smiling face at the top of each hill and was encouraged to peddle hard.

Marsha kept asking, "You okay Mona," and Lissette followed her and asked Marsha the same of her.

I was hot and happy, ecstatic, delirious with delight, proud, weepy and hungry. And yes, I was okay.

We three musketeers, Marsha, Lissette and I had stuck together the entire day and rolled into the last water stop eight miles before we headed for the home stretch.

We filled our packs with ice cold water, doused our heads under the faucet, checked each other to make sure we looked good for the finish line photos, exchanged high fives and headed south.

With only twenty minutes left to go, the excitement of the day would reach its crescendo. Marsha slid up next to me and said, "We did it Mona, we did it."

I said, "We sure did my friend. And *you* are the best wing woman anyone could ever wish for." We rolled on holding hands for a good solid minute.

Although I had spent long hours and hundreds of miles training over those past several months, I had felt as if that day was the first time I had ridden my bike since my diagnosis.

Maybe it was because that day was the high point of my journey. Two years before, I had struggled to ride every mile. I had been unaware that I was dying. I survived the last forty miles that day only because of the ten shots of a powerful antacid that had kept the monster inside my gut quiet while I finished the ride in a blur.

Almost two years later, I was forty pounds thinner. I was healthier, happier and stronger than ever before. I was mentally, emotionally, physically and spiritually aligned. I had confidence. And I knew my life was meant for a higher purpose.

I made a statement that day that the unimaginable could be achieved. I had been willing to dig deep. I burrowed underneath the demons that haunted me and tried to keep me from living my full potential.

I endured and I had survived.

The finish line was at the Mass Maritime Academy in Bourne, one half mile off from the main road. As the three of us turned off Route 6, and turned onto the side road, hundreds of people applauded thunderously. They lined the street and cheered every rider, known or unknown.

We had no idea where my family and friends would be standing. I turned to Marsha and asked, "Do you see them?" At that moment I heard familiar voices yelling,

"Here they come. There's Denise. Here comes Auntie Denise." Just ahead on the right I noticed a huge sign that towered above the crowd. In the center of the poster was a photo of me singing at Fenway Park. The photo was surrounded by the words, "Congratulations! You did it! Hip Hip Hooray! We love you!"

I was the first to reach the gang. Before I was able to dismount Millie, I was smothered with hugs and kisses and more kisses and more hugs. To see their beautiful, happy faces was the highlight of my day. This day was as much for them as it was me. They had witnessed my transformation from a frail cancer patient to now a victorious rider.

Everyone was crying. When I saw Johnny crying it sent me sobbing. As he hugged me, he looked down and saw the photo of me and Karen taped to the top of my bike bag.

He said, "When I saw you coming I could see her sitting on your shoulder. I didn't know she was riding up front on your handle bars."

I thought if I had ridden hard enough and prayed long enough, somehow Karen would be among the crowd. I guess in some way she had been, because each of us had carried a piece of her in our hearts.

It was a while before the other Dream Team members crossed the finish line, so we parked our bikes, we filled our packs with fresh water, and joined the crowd and we cheered for each rider that passed by.

We honored them not only for that day's accomplishment but also for their personal triumphs. Whether they had ridden as a survivor or with a prayer in their heart that their efforts may have helped someone they love survive, we celebrated them equally.

Over those past two years I had been poked, prodded, devastated and delighted. I had been terrified and transformed. I questioned whether or not I would make it through alive and I celebrated the days when I felt so alive.

I had learned a new appreciation for life and how to live totally in the moment.

I learned surrender didn't mean give up; it meant open up.

I had forgiven. Mostly myself, for anything and everything.

I realized that loving myself unconditionally was a more peaceful way to live.

I celebrated the joy of being able to swallow and had a newfound appreciation for saliva. I absolutely loved the sound of my own voice, especially when I sang.

I would do it all over again because life is precious.

And the unwavering truth about life is, people get you through and love is all that matters.

I Love My Life

Each day is a gift, and each day I open this gift with a heart full of gratitude.

In September of 2007, I began ministerial school at ChIME.

Cancer had softened me, and it had also opened the door to my ministry. ChIME helped me walk through that door into my inner sanctuary that was already filled with light, love, joy, peace and many soft places to land. In my inner sanctuary I could sit with me, inspire me, support and love me, so I could then turn and face outward, and share my authentic self with the world.

For my internship I chose to work with women in prison, and I fell in love with the work. If not for ChIME I would have never traveled that road. Those women taught me much more than I could have ever taught them.

For my senior project I created a multi-media DVD/CD presentation called "Pray Peace." My intention for creating "Pray Peace" was to build bridges and break down barriers. I professionally recorded nine tracks of original music, and took the words of the peace prayers from different religions, and as a voice for peace, I spoke the prayers over the music tracks. I then created a powerful visual accompaniment of 85 slides of people, places and situations from around the globe that some of us may hold in judgment.

It does not matter what our religious beliefs are. What matters is how much tolerance and respect we have for one another's beliefs. It's time to be curious instead of judgmental and it's time to celebrate our differences.

I believe, deep in the heart of every human being lives a desire for peace. I speak from personal experience when I say, "The more peaceful we feel, the healthier we are."

In June 2009 I was ordained an Interfaith Minister.

The Pan Mass Challenge yearbook from 2007 did a feature article on me about the great events of that year. And the Red Sox just happened to win the 2007 World Series.

In 2009, SPOHNC Magazine, a magazine for people with head and neck cancer, asked me to write an article for them which went out to 17,000 members. In 2010 Unity Magazine featured a four page article on me in their New Year edition which was distributed to over 50,000. And when Michael Douglas was diagnosed with throat and neck cancer, I did a television segment for Inside Edition to help educate people about this type of cancer.

All these were opportunities that the universe orchestrated for me to be able to spread my inspirational message further, and minister to people, one on one, across the country who are dealing with cancer.

I have traveled the country from San Francisco to Maine, south to Florida and west to Santa Fe and several places in between, sharing my message of self love. Inviting people to embrace their cancer and learn from it as opposed to "battling it." I also teach my "Make a Joyful Noise" sound healing workshops to assist people in clearing out the blockages that might be in the way of their loving themselves unconditionally. And my "Pray Peace" work continues to make a significant impact on audiences where I share this powerful message.

Each and every Fall I spend at least three weeks visiting my village of Paciano, Italy. I harvest grapes, pick figs, drink vino and enjoy many Italian treats with my newly adopted Italian family.

Throughout this time I managed to find time to write this book.

I do not know what the future holds, but then again none of us knows.

But I do know one thing: God *always* shines the light on the perfect and right path for me. My part in all of it is to walk softly on this path, to pay attention, to surrender and trust. And most of all stay present to love.

Resources

ChIME
PO Box 3833
Portland, ME 04104
207-347-6740
www.chimeofmaine.org

Dr. G. Savastio
Human Nature Natural Health
Portsmouth, NH
603-610-7778
www.humannaturenaturalhealth.com

Head and Neck Cancer Alliance
PO Box 21688
Charleston, SC 29413
86-792-4622
www.headandneck.org

Marc Clopton (Shaman)
The Tannery
Mill #1-Suite 5
Newburyport, MA 01950
978-465-1229
www.newburyportacting.org

SPOHNC
Support for people with Oral Head and Neck Cancer
PO Box 53
Locust Valley, NY 11560
800-377-0928
www.spohnc.org

Tom Tam
15 Cottage Ave.
Quincy, MA 02169
617-282-2750
www.tomtam.com

Unity
1901 NW Blue Parkway
Unity Village, MO 64065
816-524-3550
www.unity.org

Unity on the River
58 Macy Street
Amesbury, MA 01930
978-834-7830
www.unityontheriver.org

BIBLIOGRAPHY

Gibran, Kahlil. *The Prophet*. Knopf 1923

Rosemergy, Jim. *Even Mystics Have Bills to Pay*. Unity Press, 2000

Tolle, Ekhart. *A New Earth*. Namaste Publishing 2005

ALSO BY DENISE DeSIMONE

Walk With Me
A CD of original music

Make a Joyful Noise
A mediation CD using sound healing

Pray Peace CD & DVD
A music & multi-media offering of personal and global peace

denise@denisedesimone.com - www.denisedesimone.com
www.fromstage4tocenterstage.com